Cultural Astronomy of the Japanese Archipelago

Goto introduces the diverse and multilayered skylore and cultural astronomy of the peoples of the Japanese Archipelago.

Going as far back as the Jomon, Yayoi, and Kofun periods, this book examines the significance of constellations in the daily life of farmers, fishermen, sailors, priests, and the ruling classes throughout Japan's ancient and medieval history. As well as covering the systems of the dominant Japanese people, he also explores the astronomy of the Ainu people of Hokkaido, and of the people of the Ryukyu Islands. Along the way he discusses the importance of astronomy in official rituals, mythology, and Shinto and Buddhist ceremonies.

This book provides a unique overview of cultural astronomy in Japan and is a valuable resource for researchers as well as anyone who is interested in Japanese culture and history.

Akira Goto is Professor of Anthropology at Nanzan University, Japan. Born in 1954, Sendai, Japan, Professor Goto obtained his B.A. and M.A. from University of Tokyo (archaeology), followed by his Ph.D. in anthropology from University of Hawai'i. He was also the director of Anthropological Institute, Nanzan University from 2010–2018.

Routledge Studies in the Early History of Asia

4 **The Diary of a Manchu Soldier in Seventeenth-Century China**
 "My Service in the Army", by Dzengeo
 Introduction, Translation and Notes by Nicola Di Cosmo

5 **Past Human Migrations in East Asia**
 Matching Archaeology, Linguistics and Genetics
 Edited by Alicia Sanchez-Mazas, Roger Blench, Malcolm D. Ross, Ilia Peiros and Marie Lin

6 **Rethinking the Prehistory of Japan**
 Language, Genes and Civilisation
 Ann Kumar

7 **Ancient Chinese Encyclopedia of Technology**
 Jun Wenren

8 **Women and the Literary World in Early Modern China, 1580–1700**
 Daria Berg

9 **Asian Expansions**
 The Historical Experiences of Polity Expansion in Asia
 Edited by Geoff Wade

10 **The Emergence of Civilizational Consciousness in Early China**
 History Word by Word
 Uffe Bergeton

11 **Cultural Astronomy of the Japanese Archipelago**
 Exploring the Japanese Skyscape
 Akira Goto

Cultural Astronomy of the Japanese Archipelago
Exploring the Japanese Skyscape

Akira Goto

LONDON AND NEW YORK

First published in English 2021
by Routledge
2 Park Square, Milton Park, Abingdon, Oxon OX14 4RN

and by Routledge
52 Vanderbilt Avenue, New York, NY 10017

Routledge is an imprint of the Taylor & Francis Group, an informa business

© 2021 Akira Goto

The right of Akira Goto to be identified as author of this work has been asserted by him in accordance with sections 77 and 78 of the Copyright, Designs and Patents Act 1988.

All rights reserved. No part of this book may be reprinted or reproduced or utilized in any form or by any electronic, mechanical, or other means, now known or hereafter invented, including photocopying and recording, or in any information storage or retrieval system, without permission in writing from the publishers.

Trademark notice: Product or corporate names may be trademarks or registered trademarks, and are used only for identification and explanation without intent to infringe.

British Library Cataloguing-in-Publication Data
A catalogue record for this book is available from the British Library

Library of Congress Cataloging-in-Publication Data
A catalog record for this book has been requested

ISBN: 978-0-367-40798-8 (hbk)
ISBN: 978-0-367-80912-6 (ebk)

Typeset in Times New Roman
by Wearset Ltd, Boldon, Tyne and Wear

Contents

List of figures vi
List of tables viii

Introduction 1

1 Japanese people and stars: cultural astronomy and star lore of the Japanese 8

2 Stars in mythology and classical literature 24

3 Star lore of the Hokkaido Ainu 38

4 Ethnoastronomy in the Ryukyu Islands 48

5 Archaeoastronomy of prehistoric Japan: a historical survey 63

6 Fallen star legends in Japanese folk beliefs 89

7 Cosmology seen in house and burial orientation of the Hokkaido Ainu, northern Japan 103

8 The sun and the Kingdom of Ryukyu: an ethnohistorical approach to state formation 121

9 Epilogue 139

Index 141

Figures

1.1	Japanese Archipelago and regions referred to in this book	8
1.2	Daishogun ("Great General") Shrine 大将軍神社 in Kyoto, where Seven-Days Stars are worshiped and a charm with a seven stars design	11
1.3	*Hagun-sho* (or *sei*) statue at Hoshida Myoken Temple 星田妙見神社 in Osaka	12
1.4	*Hagoita*, a racket for Japanese badminton	15
1.5	*Mokko*, a basket used in fishing villages	16
1.6	*Kadomatsu*, with New Year's decorations in front of Saiho-ji Temple 西方寺, Miyagi Prefecture (December, 2015)	8
2.1	Sumiyoshi Shrine 住吉神社 in Osaka	28
2.2	Constellations supposed to correspond to the myth of "The August Descent from Heaven" (Katsumata 2000, frontispiece)	30
2.3	Fujiwara Kyo Capital and surrounding mountains	35
2.4	Kitano Tenmangu Shrine and "Three Lights Gate"	36
3.1	Map of Hokkaido	38
3.2	Sacred Altar dedicated by *inaw*	40
3.3	*Sapanpe* (*inaw* crowns) exhibited in the Ainu Cultural Museum, Biratori	43
4.1	Map of Ryukyu Islands	48
4.2	Misaki Utaki, Taketomi Island, Yaeyama Archipelago	53
4.3	*Shichi-sadame Ishi*, Kohama Island, Yaeyama Archipelago	55
4.4	*Hoshi-mi-ishi* in Yaeyama Archipelago	55
4.5	Muribushi-Utaki, Ishigaki Island	56
4.6	Star chart, Hateruma Island	60
4.7	Sun stone, Kume Island	61
5.1	June Solstice sunrise from Futamiga-ura, Ise (June 22, 2017)	65
5.2	Burial orientation in Hokkaido Sites	68

5.3	Burial orientation at Sanganji Site	70
5.4	Burial orientation at Genjodaira Site	71
5.5	Oyu Stone Circle	72
5.6	Oshoro Stone Circle	73
5.7	Hirabaru site, Fukuoka	75
5.8	Yoshinogari site, Saga	77
5.9	Orientation of Kofun burial	79
5.10	Star charts of Soshoku Kofun in Asuka	81
5.11	Stone monuments in Asuka	83
6.1	Map of western Japan	91
6.2	Shrines and Temples in Kudamatsu City related to fallen star legends	92
6.3	Monuments, Shrines, and Temples in Katano City related to fallen star legends	94
6.4	Shrines and Temples related to fallen star legend in Bisei Towan	95
6.5	Hoshi Jinja Shrine in Okayama City	97
6.6	Shrines related to fallen star legends in Imabari City and Nihama City	98
7.1	Hokkaido and its regions mentioned in this chapter	103
7.2	Prehistoric chronology of Hokkaido and Honshu (Japan's main island)	104
7.3	Ainu House (chise)	105
7.4	Archaeological sites mentioned in this chapter	109
7.5	Estimated orientation of the sacred window in house sites with an entrance chamber	110
7.6	House sites with an entrance chamber in Karinba 3 site	110
7.7	Ethnographic example of Tokachi Ainu House	111
7.8	Burial orientation of Pre-Modern Ainu, Modern Ainu, and Okhotsk Periods	115
7.9	Accumulation of bear skulls in the pit dwelling site at Moyoro Shell Mound Museum (an annex of Abashiri City Municipal Museum)	116
8.1	Okinawa Main Island and archaeological sites and monuments mentioned in this chapter	122
8.2	Naka Gusuku Castle	124
8.3	Tamagusuku Castle	125
8.4	Urasoe Castle and Kudaka Island	127
8.5	Urasoe Youdore	129
8.6	Kudaka Island	131
8.7	Shuri Castle	133
8.8	Seifa-Utaki	135

Tables

4.1	Heliacal rise and acoustic rise of stars, Tarama Island (based on Kuroshima 1999)	58
4.2	Rise and set directions of stars (based on Kuroshima 1999)	59
7.1	Burial orientation by local Ainu group of the Pre-Modern Ainu period (based on Utagawa 2004b)	114

Introduction

Although there are quite a few studies of cultural astronomy in Japan, the scope of research so far has been limited. The most popular subfield of cultural astronomy has been paleo-astronomy 古天文学, which is the study of ancient (and often abnormal) astronomical phenomena identified in relation to those that actually occurred using calculation and simulation. Saito Kuniji was one of the pioneers of this field and his work remains popular today (e.g., Saito 1982, 1990).

Another field of cultural astronomy that has been well researched is the study of religious beliefs of Esoteric Buddhism introduced from China. In Esoteric Buddhism, such as the Shingon Mission 真言宗 and the Tendai Mission 天台宗, astrological rituals have been practiced and these beliefs syncretized with Yin-Yo Theory Onmyodo 陰陽道. These thoughts have also been expressed in fine arts, such as the Star Mandara 星曼荼羅. In addition, the principal text of the Nichiren Mission 日蓮宗, *Kokuzo-Gumonji-Ho* 『虚空蔵求聞持法』, associates Venus with Kokuzo-Bosatsu 虚空蔵菩薩 Ākāśagarbhāya and this belief is distributed widely as an aspect of folk religion (Sano 1994).

In many Esoteric Buddhist temples and the Nichren Mission, star festivals 星祭り have been held on particular days of the year and are still practiced today (Sano 1994). These religious practices, however, are not held to actually observe stars, since these religions concerned with stars have been developed on the basis of religious thoughts that already had been established in China or the Korean Peninsula. Therefore, the introduction of these ideas did not lead to the observation of stars (Sano 1994).

This is also true of most the popular folk custom concerning stars, the *Tanabata* 七夕. This custom is held annually to celebrate the date of Kengyu 牽牛 (Altair) and Shukujo 織女 (Vega) across the Amanogawa 天の川 (Milky Way). The date should be the seventh day in the seventh month of the lunar calendar when a waxing crescent moon is to be seen as a boat crossing the river (Milky Way). Although Japanese children decorate bamboo branches with beautiful paper and votive paper splits, today they do not seem to be actually praying for stars. Thus, *Tanabata* has not been held to observe stars but to practice as a step toward the *Omon* Festival お盆 when people welcome ancestral spirits (Renshaw 2011).

Japanese practices observe the moon more than stars or the sun. This tendency is seen in many poems in classical Japanese literature, such as the *Manyoshu* 万葉集 (*Collection of Ten Thousand Leaves*). Also, the custom of *Otsukimi* お月見, or "watching the moon," is still practiced today. This is held on the fifteenth day of the eighth month in the lunar calendar in order to praise the full moon by offering rice dumplings with fruits.

Although studies of cultural astronomy related to Esoteric Buddhism, Buddhist fine arts, and the *Tanabata* custom have been well documented, they are outside the scope of this book. In contrast, this book mainly aims to discuss how people in the Japanese Archipelago have observed and conceived of the stars and the universe, and how the people have used knowledge of stars for everyday life.

In this book, I often use the term "Japanese Archipelago" instead of "Japan." Since "Japan" is a political term that masks the nation's cultural diversity, I intentionally use the geographical term "Japanese Archipelago" to emphasize the diverse traditions that exist in the region's cultural astronomical practices.

Since the Japanese Archipelago consists of a long chain of islands running from north to south, and also from east to west, the geographical conditions of the archipelago have created diverse ways of using astronomical phenomena for practical purposes. In addition, Japan's long history has incorporated different cultural and religious factors into its star lore, such as Chinese influences, Buddhist influences, Shinto beliefs, and several others.

Concerning Japanese transcription in this book, I consistently express Japanese names in the following order: family name and then given name, regardless of whether the person mentioned is a historical figure or not.

In the first four chapters, I will present an overview of star lore, such as vernacular star names, myths, and legends of stars in the Japanese Archipelago. There is significant variation on the visibility of stars along the long north-south chain of the Japanese Archipelago. Japan's northernmost island, Hokkaido, is home to an indigenous hunter–gatherer population called the Ainu, who have developed a rich star lore. On the other hand, in the southernmost islands, the Ryukyu Islands, the Okinawan people inherited a star lore different from that which is found in the main Japanese islands. I will discuss the cultural astronomy of both Hokkaido and the

Ryukyu Islands together to show the diversity of the conception of the sky and the universe in the Japanese Archipelago.

Chapter 1 discusses vernacular star names and the practical use of astronomical phenomena for farming, fishing, sailing, warfare, and other purposes. This chapter aims to discuss how ordinary people (farmers, fishermen, sailors, etc.) observed stars and how these people have used these observations for everyday life, such as determining dates and physical orientations. The study of this kind of star lore has been pioneered by Nojiri Hoei and several other researchers. In particular, folklorist Kitao Koichi has published an encyclopedia of vernacular star names throughout Japan by supplementing Nojiri's works (see references in Chapter 1). In this book, I will overview star lore among Japanese ordinary people on the basis of these works.

Chapter 2 deals with astronomical topics in ancient mythology and classical literature. Although there is little clear evidence that deities in Japanese mythology symbolized stars, I will explore this possibility to interpret some myths that were the result of astronomical phenomena. The highest goddess of Japanese mythology, *Amaterasu Ohmikami* 天照大神, is thought to symbolize the sun, and her brother, *Tsukuyomi-no-mikoto* 月読尊, symbolizes the moon. In Ise Shrine, where *Amaterasu* is worshiped, the sacred object is a mirror that symbolizes the shinning of the sun and there is an opinion that the *tenson korin* 天孫降臨 (the descent to earth of the grandson of *Amaterasu*) myth is expressed in heaven by constellations raging from Pleiades, Taurus, and Orion.

In Chapter 3, I discuss the vernacular star names and beliefs among the Ainu. This chapter demonstrates how the Ainu people were using stars to cope with seasonal variation in natural resources. I will also examine the Ainu people's concept of an afterworld and cosmology in relation to astronomical phenomena. This chapter will show that Ainu people's myths of stars and cosmology are comparable with ethnic groups in northern Eurasia and America.

Chapter 4 discusses the characteristics of vernacular star names and the indigenous astronomy of the Okinawan people. One of the most important aspects of Ryukyu Island religion is that there was little influence of either Buddhism or Shintoism, and traditional belief and oral history in the Ryukyu Islands possibly retain some aspects of ancient elements of Japanese culture before the influence of Buddhism. In this chapter, I will demonstrate unique aspects of Ryukyu cultural astronomy in Japan, including the mythology and legends concerning astronomy, star maps, star charts, the sunstone, star (Pleiades) observing stones, a Pleiades shrine, and others.

The next four chapters discuss more specific issues in cultural astronomy in the Japanese Archipelago.

Chapter 5 is a historical review of archaeoastronomy in Japan. I will present a variety of archaeoastronomical research that has been conducted and discuss the unique history of Japanese archaeoastronomy. After the modernization of Japan in 1868, western scholars, such as William Gowland and Neil Munro, played an important role in developing academic disciplines, which marked the earliest attempt at archaeoastronomy in Japan. Stimulated by these British scholars, Japanese archaeologists started to pursue archaeoastronomical studies, such as examining burial orientations, the alignment of stone circles of the Jomon Period, the orientation of *kofun* 古墳 (tumuli), and others. During the professionalization of archaeology after World War II, however, archaeoastronomical interests diminished except for a few researchers and amateurs who have explored these areas over the past 50 years. Only recently has the interest in archaeoastronomy has been revived by researchers, including myself. This chapter describes a somewhat "strange history of archaeoastronomy" in Japan (cf. Hutton 2013) and reports recent research in this field from the Jomon 13,000 BCE) to the Asuka Period (seventh to eighth centuries).

Chapter 6 analyzes fallen star legends found mainly in western Japan. In particular, this chapter discusses how heavenly phenomena have materialized on earth. In western Japan, there are several Shinto shrines and Buddhist temples whose objects of worship are said to be the remnant of fallen stars, such as meteorites. This belief is certainly related to Esoteric Buddhism and probably the activity of ironsmiths: the technology of smiths that use fire is often considered to have originated in heaven and astronomical phenomena strongly influence mineral phenomenon (cf. Milcea Eliade, *The Forge and the Crucible: The Origins and Structure of Alchemy*). This chapter traces the formation of fallen star legends in a socioeconomic context.

Chapter 7 analyzes the orientation of dwelling and burials among the Pre-Modern Ainu. The orientation of houses and burials seem to have been decided based on several factors, such as the direction of the sunrise/sunset, river orientations, land slopes, and various others. Ainu villages were typically arranged along a river and the river's upstream movement toward a sacred mountain was just as important as the orientation of the sun. This indicates that we should develop a more integrated view of the ways the Ainu understand nature and orientation in order to increase our comprehension of these questions.

Chapter 8 analyzes the development of solar ideology in the Ryukyu Kingdom in relation to folk beliefs among the Okinawan people. On Okinawa Island, the largest island of the chain, the Kingdom of Shuri was established around the fifteenth century. Its political ideology was characterized by sun rituals and the king was worshiped as a child of the sun. In this chapter, I trace the process in which primary folk belief in the sun had been transformed into a political ideology whereby the king became the sun, radiating the land and the people.

Thus, there is a rich tradition of cultural astronomy in the Japanese Archipelago. Delayed research in these areas has resulted not from a paucity of cultural astronomical activity but from unawareness and lack of interest among researchers (Renshaw and Ihara 2000). Fortunately, in accord with the recent trend of cultural astronomy in the international context (Selin 2000; Ruggles 2015), interest in cultural astronomy seems to have been recently renewed in various research fields. In accordance with this trend, research grants have been offered to interdisciplinary projects in which archaeologists, ethnologists, anthropologists, mythologists, astronomers, and researchers of related fields cooperate. I hope this small book serves as a turning point to revitalize and promote this trend among both Japanese and non-Japanese researchers.

This book is a product of the following grants that I have obtained in the last seven years as a research representative and also grants I am currently participating in as a co-investigator.

The grants Grant-in-Aid for Scientific Research (KAKENHI) 科研費 I used for completing this book are as follows:

1. The Establishment of Anthropological Astronomy as Neo-Science: Grant-in-Aid for Scientific Research (C), 2014–2016 [Kekenhi 26370967]; Goto Akira as Principal Investigator.
2. The Planetarium as Demonstration Space of Anthropology–Diversity of Cultural Astronomy in Japan: Grant-in-Aid for Scientific Research (C), 2017–2019 [Kakenhi 17K03299.]; Goto Akira as Principal Investigator.
3. The Establishment of Cooperation between Archaeology, History and Astronomy: Grant-in-Aid for Scientific Research (A), 2019–2022 [Kakenhi 19H00544], Hojo Yoshitaka as Principal Investigator; Goto Akira as Co-Investigator.
4. Monument and the Establishment of Spatio-Temporal Framework: Grant-in-Aid for Scientific Research on Innovative Areas (Comparative Study of Out-of-Eurasia Civilizations: Matsumoto Naoko as Research Representative), 2019–2023 [Kakenhi 19H05732]; Tsurumi Eisei as Principal Investigator; Goto Akira as Co-Investigator.

Acknowledgments

I would like to thank the following institutes and publishers for permitting me to use their photos and figures in this book: Abashiri City Municipal Museum, Doseisha, Eniwa City Board of Education, Fukushima Prefectural

Museum, Gakuseisha, Kinokuniya-shoten, Kayano Shigeru Nibutani Ainu Museum, Kitano Tenmangu Temple, Kodansha, Kyobunkan, Kyoto Sangyo University, Nibutani Ainu Culture Museum, Okinawa Churashima Foundation, Okinawa Prefecture Board of Education, Shibetsu Town Board of Education, Taishukan, Yaeyama Museum, and Yuzankaku.

I am also especially grateful to the following individuals who kindly granted me permission to use photos and figures from their work: Arakawa Hiroshi, Hojo Yoshitaka, Izumi Takeshi, Katsumata Takashi, Kitao Koichi, Sago, Tsutomu, Tsujita Junichiro, and Uchida Yuichi.

I would also like to thank the National Astronomical Observatory of Japan (NAOJ) for offering me the opportunity to conduct several stimulating workshops. In addition, Nanzan University also deserves gratitude for always providing a comfortable research atmosphere.

In addition, I am grateful to NPO Okinwa Denshowa Shiryo Center (Okinawa Oral History Research Center) and late Endo Shoji who founded this center, for providing unpublished folk tales in the Ryukyu Islands.

The following colleagues and research collaborators of my KAKENHI research grant deserve significant gratitude for their cooperation and useful discussions: Aihara Kazuharu, Ishimura Tomo, Konno Toshiaki, Monden Osamu, Takuya, Onishi Hieyuki, Oku Tomoki, Sunami Soichiro, Suganuma Ayano, Takao Toru, and Yoshida Fumi.

Simon Bates of Routledge Asia is owed a special word of thanks for providing an opportunity for me to write this book.

Finally, great thanks go to Paul Capobianco, who read the draft many times and always gave me insightful advice for revisions.

References

Hutton, Ronald
    2013   The strange history of British archaeoastronomy. *Journal for the Study of Religion, Nature and Culture* 7(4): 376–397.

Renshaw, Steven L.
    2011   Celebration of seasonally based holidays and festivals in Japan: a study in cultural adaptation. In: C. Ruggles (ed.), *Archaeoastronoy and Ethnoastronoy: Building Bridges between Cultures*, pp. 308–314. Cambridge: Cambridge University Press.

Renshaw, Steven L. and Saori Ihara
    2000   A cultural history of astronomy in Japan. In: H. Selin (ed.), *Astronomy Across Cultures: the History of Non-Western Astronomy*, pp. 385–407. New York: Springer.

Ruggles, Clive (ed.)
    2015   *Handbook of Archaeoastronomy and Ethnoastronomy*, 3 Volumes. New York: Springer.

Saito, Kuniji 斉藤国治
- 1982 *The Astronomy of the Asuka Period.*『飛鳥時代の天文学』Tokyo: Kawade Shobo.
- 1990 *A Road to Palaeoastronomy.*『古天文学への道』Tokyo: Hara Shobo.

Sano, Kenji 佐野賢治
- 1994 An introduction to the history of worship of star gods in Japan: focused on Myoken and Kokuzo Bosatsu beliefs.「日本神星信仰史概論: 妙見 虚空蔵信仰 を中心にして」In: K. Sano (ed.), *Belief of Stars: Myoken and Kokuzo*『星の信仰: 妙見 虚空蔵』, pp. 3–53. Tokyo: Keisuisha.

Selin, Helaine (ed.)
- 2000 *Astronomy across Cultures: the History of Non-Western Astronomy.* Dordrecht: Kluwer Academic Publishers.

1 Japanese people and stars
Cultural astronomy and star lore of the Japanese

Astronomy in the Japanese Archipelago

The seasonality of subsistence activities differs between the north and south of the Japanese Archipelago (Figure 1.1). Most of the islands of Japan belong to a temperate zone that has four seasons. On the other hand, the northernmost island, Hokkaido, belongs to a cold temperate or sub-Arctic

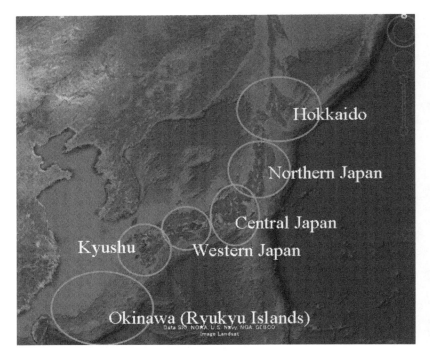

Figure 1.1 Japanese Archipelago and regions referred to in this book.

climate zone, and the southernmost islands, the Ryukyu Islands, belong to a sub-tropical zone. In astronomy, the difference in latitude defines the visibility of constellations and the use of particular constellations for season reckoning could differ by region.

The east-west extension of the archipelago has created considerable differences in the rising setting times of the sun, moon, and other constellations. For instance, the sunrise in June solstice differs approximately two hours between eastern Hokkaido and Okinawa Prefecture.

In addition, the Japanese Archipelago is home to diverse cultural traditions. In Hokkaido, there is an indigenous hunter–gatherer group, the Ainu, who have a rich star lore tradition (Sueoka 1979). Their lore is mainly based on animism and has some similarities to that of ethnic groups in northeast Asia (Sueoka 1979: 32–33) (see Chapter 3 for further discussion).

In the south, the Ryukyu Kingdom maintained independence until the beginning of the seventeenth century. Buddhism and Shintoism have scarcely influenced religious traditions of this region and the Ryukyu Islanders have maintained local shamanism until today. Their lore is built upon a mixture of Chinese, Japanese, and indigenous traditions, which likely include some Austronesian elements (Goto 2011; Nojiri 1973: 182). The Ryukyu Islanders used indigenous star charts and star books for season-reckoning and navigation (see Chapter 4 for further discussion).

In the "middle" of Japan, there is a culture with a long history influenced by China and Korea. Here, the star lore and cosmology developed based on the mixture of Buddhism, Shintoism, Confucianism, and indigenous animistic folk beliefs. This region is divided into northern Japan (e.g., Tohoku), central Japan (e.g., Kanto and Chubu), western Japan (e.g., Kansai, Chugoku, and Shikoku Island), and Kyushu Island.

As will be shown, Japanese farmers have used several stars to determine the appropriate seasons for agricultural activities, such as rice farming. An essayist of the Edo Period, Hata Kakuzan, who lived during the mid-eighteenth to mid-nineteenth centuries, wrote in his essay *Yomo-no-suzuri* 『四方の硯』:

> Nobody observes stars better than farmers. Since Yamato County (Nara Prefecture) is poor in water, farmers, from April to summer, without sleeping, observe only stars in order to plant rice. Also, they check the moisture of rice crops by observing morning dew in order to predict its harvest. They named those stars *karasuki-boshi* (Chinese plow star: Orion), *hishi-boshi* (diamond-shape star: Cassiopeia), *subaru-boshi* (Pleiades), *kudo-boshi*, and so on. They carefully observe the time of their rising, their altitude, and setting points, and their estimates never failed.
>
> (Kanezashi 1974: 18)

In addition, although there is only fragmentary information concerning indigenous navigation, Japanese navigation was mainly based on the *yama-ate* method, which means "addressing mountains." This involves observing two mountains to locate your position in the sea. There is evidence, however, that stars were also used for navigation. In *Hiyorimiyo* 『和見様』, the weather forecasting book written by the pirates of Setouchi Inland Sea, the Nojima Navy 野嶋水軍 (around the sixteenth century) mentioned that the Big Dipper, Polaris, the Orion, and the Pleiades could be used for knowing direction and the weather.

In what follows, I will introduce the vernacular names of several conspicuous stars and their relevant beliefs and customs. It has been thought that Japanese people were poor observers of stars, but I will show that Japanese farmers, fishermen, and sailors had a rich custom of observing stars for their subsistence.

Star lore among Japanese populations

The Big Dipper

The Big Dipper is the most conspicuous constellation throughout the archipelago, as it is seen in many months of the year. There are several local names of the Big Dipper: *kaji-boshi* is one that means "a rudder star." Here, the Big Dipper appeared to be a rudder of the ship when it lied vertically. The Big Dipper was also called *funa-boshi*, which means "a ship star," signifying five stars in a square, which looked as if it was a ship.

Minamoto Yoshitsune 源義経, a famous *samurai* warrior in the twelfth century was written to have said, "I was lost at sea because I could not see *shi-so no hoshi*." *Shi-so* means "four and three," indicating four stars in the rise and three stars in the handle. This episode suggests that the Big Dipper was important to fishermen and sailors from the Medieval Period.

There was a proverb told among fishermen: *shi-so-no-hosi* turns around *kitano-hitotsu-boshi*, which literally means "One Star in the North (the Polaris)," in order to eat it. In order to protect the "One Star in the North," *yarai-boshi* (*yarai* = fence against arrows) is turning, more closely around Polaris. *Yarai-boshi* corresponds to two stars: β and γ of the Little Dipper. This proverb indicates that the people on the sea paid attention to Polaris and the movement of the Big Dipper in order to know the direction and the passage of time (Nojiri 1973: 3–14).

In most parts of Japan, the Big Dipper has often been mentioned in relation to the belief in the Bodhisattva *Myoken* 妙見菩薩 (Arichi 2006).

Myoken is a personification of the Polar Star and the Big Dipper and is called *hokuto-shichisei*, or "seven stars in the north." Since the Big Dipper is going around Polaris, belief in *Myoken* and in *Hokuto* have often been merged into one. Belief in *Hokuto* was also important among samurai groups in the Medieval and Early Modern periods (Kanezashi 1971) (Figure 1.2).

The seven stars were perceived as seven deities in the pantheon of the Esoteric universe. According to the Buddhistic sutra that mentions the 7 stars, each of the stars was designated as the personal guardian star according to the 12 zodiac signs under which people were born. This belief was a fusion of astronomy, astrology, Esoteric Buddhism, and Chinese zodiac traditions: *Donro-sho* (Alkaid) signifying the rat; *Komon-sho* (Mizar) signifying the ox and wild boar; *Rokuzon sho* (Alioth) signifying the tiger and dog; *Mongoku-sho* (Megrez) signifying the rabbit and rooster; *Renchosho* (Phecda) signifying the dragon and monkey; *Mugoku-sho* (Merek) signifying the snake and sheep; and *Hagun-sho* (Dubhe) signifying the horse (Arichi 2006; Kanezashi 1974: 183) (Figure 1.3).

The last of these, *Hagun-sho* (or *sei*) 破軍星, literally means "the star to break the enemy's forces" and was particularly important to the *samurai* clans in battle. They predicted outcomes by observing which direction this star was pointing. In a similar way, the Big Dipper was considered important for gamblers; it was believed that if you were betting when the Big Dipper was visible above you, you would win (Nojiri 1958: 7–10). The importance of the Big Dipper among fishermen, sailors, warriors, and gamblers may derive from the same line of magical thinking concerning the position and direction of this constellation.

Figure 1.2 Daishogun ("Great General") Shrine 大将軍神社 in Kyoto, where Seven-Days Stars are worshiped and a charm with a seven stars design.

Figure 1.3 Hagun-sho (or *sei*) statue at Hoshida Myoken Temple 星田妙見神社 in Osaka.

Bootes and Corvus

Farmers of the Setouchi Inland Sea in western Japan sowed wheat when *mugi-boshi* (the wheat-star), Arcturus, rose in the eastern sky at dawn around November. They harvested wheat when this star sat on the western horizon at dawn around mid-May. Here, the red color of Arcturus was associated with reddish ripe wheat.

In northern Japan, Arcturus was called *hato-boshi*, meaning "pigeon star." When the cold north wind ended, and late spring arrived, a big orange star appeared over the eastern mountain during the evening. This specified the season when mountain pigeons would fly down and disturb the garden (Nojiri 1973: 26–27).

In Lake Hamanako of central Japan, Arcturus was called *kaji-kai boshi*. The farmers changed the water in rice paddies when this star reached the mountain in the west during midnights of July. Since *kaji-kai-boshi* sounds like "rudder-paddle-star," this name may have derived from fishermen who used this star for knowing the fishing season or for navigation. For instance, Arcturus was used among fishermen of the Setouchi Inland Sea to determine the appropriate season for catching shrimp octopus, goby, and crab. It was there called *uojima-boshi* (a fish-island star), which indicates the start of the season of abundant fish (Uchida 1973: 157–165).

Throughout Japan, the rectangular shape of Corvus was called *hokake-boshi*, meaning a "sail-shape star." This name was probably used among the sailors of *kitamae-bune*, a north-bound ship route that transported products from Hokkaido Island to western Japan during the Edo Period (1600–1868). Since *kitamae-bune* was sailed frequently and by many ships, this name spread to other places as well (Nojiri 1958: 24).

Scorpio

When the rainy season ended around early July, a long chain of Scorpio rises vertically like a fire flame. In western Japan, it was called *yanagi-boshi* (a willow star), since it resembles a weeping willow. However, in mid-summer, Scorpio changes its position in the southern sky and looks like a fishhook. In the Setouchi Inland Sea, Scorpio was called *uotsuri-boshi* (a star for hooking fish) or *tai-tsuri-boshi* (a star for hooking sea bream). On the Japan Sea side, it was also called *katsuo-boshi*, meaning a star for *bonito* (fishing). In Okinawa, Scorpio was called *iyucha-bushi*, which means a fishhook-star (Nojiri 1973: 41–42). All of these offer comparative examples of how Japanese fishermen saw Scorpio as the shape of a fishhook, similar to the Polynesians.

There are also several interesting names for Scorpio. Antares has σ and τ stars at both sides and together these three stars were called *kagokatsugi-boshi* (a carrying-basket star), *tenbin-boshi* (a scale star), or *akindo-boshi* (a merchant star). All of these names derived from the fact that the shape of the three stars looks like a man carrying a scale with heavy baskets at both sides. Similar names could also be applied to Orion's Belt. The baggage was too heavy, which is why the man carrying them in the middle (Antares) had a red face. Antares was referred to as *aka-boshi*, literally meaning "a red star."

If the stars at both ends appeared to be lower, it was believed that the price of rice would be cheap, since the baskets were full of rice. This suggested that a good harvest was coming and that there would be an oversupply of rice. If the stars appeared to be a little higher, the price of rice would be high, since the baskets were not full of rice and therefore there would be a shortage of supply. Also, two small stars, μ1 and μ2, were called *sumotori-boshi* (*sumo* wrestler stars), since the two stars looked as if they were pushing against each other like *sumo* wrestlers (Nojiri 1973: 45–48).

The Pleiades and Hyades

Among winter stars, the Pleiades is the most conspicuous. In his fieldwork throughout Japan, Kitao has pointed out that there are two major names for Pleiades, *subaru* or *sumaru* from Honshu to the Kyushu Islands, and *muri-bushi* (clustered stars) in the islands south of Kyushu (e.g., Amami and Ryukyu Islands; see Chapter 7 for further discussion) (Kitao 2018: 16–52).

This star cluster has been called many different names, such as *azuki-boshi* (red bean stars), *gunkan-boshi* (battleship stars), and *mutsura-boshi* (six string stars) among others. It is likely that the Pleiades appeared to be a group of battleships. The Pleiades was also called *hagoita-boshi*, meaning "battledore star" (Figure 1.4). *Hagoita* is used in Japanese badminton, which is usually played during the New Year season (Nojiri 1973: 121–122; Kitao 2018: 16–98).

The Pleiades has been most important to farmers and fisherman throughout Japan for determining the seasons. For instance, the heliacal rise of the Pleiades in June was the mark of planting rice in central Japan and thus the Pleiades were called *no-boshi*, which means a "star for agriculture." This seasonality does not apply to other areas, however. For instance, rice planting was usually done in March in the Kyushu region. Planting rice also occurred early in northern Japan (May), where it is colder than in central Japan. The difference comes from the difference in temperature and hours of sunlight.

Figure 1.4 Hagoita, a racket for Japanese badminton.
Source: courtesy of Kitao Koichi.

When the Pleiades came to a zenith at dawn in September, this was the time to sow buckwheat in western Japan. There was a proverb "*subaru mandoki soba-no-toki*," meaning "when the Pleiades are in the zenith, it is a time to sow buckwheat." In central and northern Japan, acronical set of the Pleiades was the time to sow wheat (Uchida 1973: 5–8).

In Miyagi Prefecture (northern Japan), V-shaped Hyades was called *tagara-boshi*. *Tagara* is a basket carried on one's back for transporting seaweed and crops throughout this region (Chida 2015:72). Alternatively, it was called *mokko-boshi*, with *mokko* also being a local name of carrying baskets in Iwate Prefecture of northern Japan (Kitao 2001: 58–59) (Figure 1.5).

Figure 1.5 Mokko, a basket used in fishing villages.
Source: courtesy of Kitao Koichi.

Orion

Orion has been called various names: one of them is *tsutsumi-boshi*. *Tutsumi* is a Japanese traditional hand drum. The heliacal rise of Orion occurs in late July, which corresponds to *natsu-no-doyo* (the day of the summer dog). In central Japan, when the three stars appeared in the early morning, farmers went mowing. During the Bon funeral festival of the old calendar (now corresponding to August), Orion rose at 1 or 2 a.m. and this told the people to send off the spirits of the dead that were welcomed during the Bon festival (Uchida 1973: 62–65).

The culmination of Orion at dawn indicated the sowing season for buckwheat. This is probably around 5 a.m. in the middle of September. In central Japan, there was a saying that "*mitsu-boshi hiruma, kona hachigo*," meaning "when three stars are in the mid-day, eight *go* [one *go* = about 150 g] powder can be got." Here, the expression "in the mid-day" means that the stars came to a culmination. Another expression is "*sora-naka*," meaning "in the middle of the sky." Since the seasonality of Orion is close to that of the Pleiades, similar wisdom was expressed concerning the sowing buckwheat (Uchida 1973: 53–55).

Acronical set of Orion's Belt in early December was a time for sowing wheat in central and western Japan. In addition, fishermen in Fukui, western Japan, said that when *karasuki* (a Chinese plow) that is Orion rose in the evening (in the eastern sky), scads and mackerel ate well. Acronical rise of Orion was close to the winter solstice and farmers performed an important Buddhist annual rite: *sandaishi* ("three great princes") (Uchida 1973: 57–58).

Sowing wheat in December, farmers of Shizuoka, central Japan, said that "if three stars are in the direction of eastern sky near zenith, let's stop working." During this cold season, garden soil was frozen in the morning and therefore farmers sowed seeds of wheat, radish, and millet in the early evening when the soil was slightly warmer. In other places, the same custom was practiced when farmers saw the Pleiades in the western sky near its zenith.

In May, three stars appear in the western sky after the sunset. This told farmers to start working on their rice paddies. In Shizuoka, the three stars were called "*suji-kai*." Here, *suji* meant "rice species" and *kai* probably meant "star" (Uchida 1973: 60).

In the Edo Period (1600–1868), an essayist wrote that they observed that "*mitsu-twuranetaru-hosi*" reached Sado Island on the west coast of Japan. The name of this star is literally translated "a series of three stars" and this name must have referred to Orion's Belt (Katsumata 2000: 112–113). In the folklore of the Setouchi Inland Sea, Orion was called *ate-boshi*, meaning a "direction-telling star" or *nerai-boshi*, meaning a "targeting star" (Nojiri 1958: 30; Kuwahara 1963: 146).

I argue that Orion's Belt was one of the most important stars for fishermen and sailors, and this importance must have originated in ancient mythology, which will be further discussed in the next chapter.

Cassiopeia

Due to its W-shape, Cassiopeia was called *ikari-boshi*, meaning "an anchor star" in many regions. During summer nights, fishermen on the sea knew the coming of dawn, seeing the anchor star near its zenith. Also, they knew that the anchor star set in the evening around June 10 of the Old Calendar. These facts indicate that Cassiopeia was an important constellation for fishermen and sailors. In Shikoku Island of western Japan, Cassiopeia was also called *yamagata-boshi*, meaning a "mountain-shaped star." This comes from seeing Cassiopeia upside down, like the letter M.

In a religious context, Cassiopeia could be called *goyo-sei*, "five-days-star," in contrast with, *shichi-yo-sei*, "seven-days-star," which is the Big Dipper. These names came from Esoteric Buddhism and the people knew that when the "five-days-star" was visible, the "seven-days-star" is not visible, and vice versa (Nojiri 1973: 96–100).

Gemini

The time when Gemini sets at dawn in the western sky (end of January) corresponds to *daikan* (big coldness) in the Japanese traditional lunar calendar, and that is why Gemini was called *kanbosi* (cold star). When rising in the eastern sky, two major stars of Gemini, α and β, are positioned vertically, but they are seen in a parallel position in zenith and in the western sky. The two stars set in a horizontal position in the western sky, late January, when the people ate rice cakes that they had dedicated during New Year ceremonies. That is why this star was called *mochi-boshi* (rice cake star) or *mochikui-boshi* (star eating race cake) in western Japan (Nojiri 1973: 31).

Gemini was also called *monbashira* (*mon* meaning "gate," *b(h)ashira* meaning "pillar") or *kadokui* (*kado* "corner," *k [g]ui* meaning "peg") in central Japan because the vertical position of Gemini as a whole looks like a *kadomatsu*, or decorative pine branches, which is a New Year decoration (Figure 1.6). *Kadomatsu* consists of a pair of decorations with vertical

Figure 1.6 Kadomatsu, with New Year's decorations in front of Saiho-ji Temple 西方寺, Miyagi Prefecture (December, 2015).

bamboo poles and pine branches. In northern Japan, it was called *matsugui* (*matsu* means "pine tree"), and this name also derived from *kadomatsu* (Uchida 1973: 123–125).

When the two major stars aligned horizontally, they resembled the eyes of aquatic animals. In particular, the two stars reminded fishermen in western Japan of the protruding eyes of a crab or it was seen as a pair of eyes of a flounder fish or stingray in Kyushu. When Gemini set around two to three o'clock in the morning in early spring, it was a time to set octopus lines (Nojiri 1973: 32–33).

Canopus

There is little evidence that Canopus was used for navigation among fishermen. Nonetheless, it must have been seen often by the fishermen for the following reasons. Canopus of Argo is visible from Japan only for a short period. In China, Canopus was thought of as a happy star and called *kotobuki-boshi*, or "star of long life." But in Japan, Canopus is called *roujin-sei*, or "star of an old man" and this implies a bad fortune is associated with it. Since this star appears only for a short time, it is called *ouchaku-boshi* (lazy star) in western Japan. Canopus is seen only in winter, which is the season of tuna fishing. When tuna fishermen went south during the winter, they must have had a chance to see Canopus.

Fishermen of central Japan called Canopus *mera-boshi* and thought it was a sign of a hurricane. In Japan, Canopus rises only slightly above the horizon on the sea and it thereafter soon sets. This gave fishermen the impression that Canopus was a soul of the dead fisherman who harbored a grudge. Thus, fishermen believed that Canopus was the ghosts of dead fishermen from a fishing village of Chiba Prefecture, Mera, and that when it appeared there would be a strong west wind (Nojiri 1958: 162–170).

Polaris

To the Japanese sailors and fishermen who usually voyaged in the northern hemisphere, Polaris must have been used for navigation and this star has been called various names, such as *hitotsu-boshi* meaning "one star," *shin-boshi* meaning "a heart or central star," *neno-hosi* meaning "a star in the direction of *ne* (rat)." *Ne* means north according to the traditional cardinal system: 12 Payments that divide a circle into 12 segments. For instance, the direction of *uma* (horse) is south.

There is a folktale concerning Polaris. In the Edo Period, there lived a sailor whose name was Tokuzo. Tokuzo lived in Osaka and engaged in sailing in a *Kitamae-bune* (northbound ship) that transported products from Hokkaido to Osaka. During Tokuzo's absence, his wife was weaving cloth. She noticed that the Polaris moves from one crosspiece of range window to the next crosspiece, and she told this to Tokuzo. Tokuzo, knowing the secret of the Polar Star, became an expert on offshore voyages (Nojiri 1958: 30–31).

Stars for fishermen (Miyagi Prefecture)

Fishermen of Miyagi Prefecture had a rich knowledge of stars for navigation purposes, telling the seasons, or determining the time of day. Miyagi is close to the world-famous fishing grounds where the warm current, *Kuroshiwo* Current, and the cold current, *Oyashiwo* Current, meet and provide a variety of fish from both the south (e.g., tuna, mackerel, etc.) and the north (salmon, cod, etc.) (Goto 1991).

Since Miyagi Prefecture is located on the Pacific Sea side of the Tohoku area, constellations largely rise in the eastern sea and set in the western mountains. Fisherman of Watari Town mentioned the stars they used for navigation (Yanagita and Kurata 1938: 53). For departure at dawn, they observed *akeno-myojo* ("bright star at dawn," Venus), the morning star in the eastern sky. They also observed *yonakano-myojo* or *yonakano-myojin* ("bright star in the middle of night," Jupiter), and *yoino-myojo* ("bright star in the evening," Venus), in the western sky in order to navigate back to the land.

In order to come back from the sea to the land, fishermen observed *matsugui* and *sankaku*. Both of them move in the northern sky near zenith to the direction of mountains in the west. Fishermen said that *matsugui* sat in the direction of the dog (WNW) and that *sankaku* sat in the direction of the wild boar (NNW) (Nojiri 1958: 22–27).

Matsugui refers to the two stars of Gemini and *matsugui* literally means a pair of vertical poles used for New Year decorations. *Matsugui* sat after dawn (20:00–21:00) in May and this time correspond to fishing season of *sawara* or Spanish mackerel. It was called *sawara-boshi* in Shikoku Island.

It is not certain what *sankaku* (triangular) refers to. Some suggest that *sankaku* refers to the three stars (δ, ε, and η) that compose the lower body of the Canis Major (Nojiri 1958: 23; Chida 2015: 37). Since these stars set not NNW but WSW in this region, there is another possibility is that *sankaku* corresponds to Cassiopeia. Although Cassiopeia never sets in this region, it must have appeared to set behind the mountain in the west. Alternatively, it could indicate Triangulum, as its name suggests.

During fall and winter, fishermen relied on *muzura* and *sandaisho* to know the fishing seasons. *Muzura* literally means six in a row and it corresponds to the Pleiades. Fishermen of Ogatsu Town said that they started fishing squid in early fall, watching the rise of *muzura*, but that they stopped fishing when *atoboshi* ("after star") rises (Kitao 2001: 54). *Atoboshi* is a Sirius and this star was called so since it rises following the Pleiades (Chida 2015: 27, 69). *Sandaisho* means "three bosses" and it corresponds to Orion's Belt. When Orion's Belt could not be seen at dawn, it was a season to fish *ishigarei* (stone flounder) in this area.

Fishermen here also paddled north to Kinkasan Island for squid fishing at night time from late summer to early fall. For orientation and time-reckoning, they observed the successive rise of the Pleiades, Aldebaran, Orion's Belt, and Sirius in the eastern sky (Chida 2015: 116). Some fishermen also mentioned that they observed the rise of Capella before the Pleiades rise (Chida 2015: 157).

Fishermen of Kawakura Town called Venus *nagashiami-tomoshi-bosi*, which means "a star of a stern man's (master fisherman) of drift net." This refers to how master fisherman used to sit in the stern (*tomo*) of a fishing boat and watch Venus until it disappeared behind the mountains. Venus was also called *kamedori-boshi*, which means "a star for filling containers of fishing boats." Bright Venus appeared to celebrate when fishermen came back from the sea with a good catch (Chida 2015: 165–168).

Fishermen in Shichigahama Town used to tell the time for catching tuna by observing the position or angle of *nanatsu-bosi* ("seven stars"), referring to the Big Dipper (Chida 2015: 61). Additionally, they used the position of the Big Dipper to know the timing for setting and hoisting the drift net (Chida 2015: 93).

Fishermen in Utatsu Town gill-netted cod between December solstice and *daikan*. They thought that when Corvus was seen in the southern sky at around four a.m., it was the best time for cod fishing. When *futatsu-boshi* (a pair of stars), referring α and β of Gemini, sat in the western mountains at dawn, cod fishing came to the end (Chida 2015: 159).

When fishermen of Watari Town observed the rise of the Pleiades about one hour (15 degrees) above the sea horizon in the east, they knew that salmon would come back to the Abukuma River. When Orion's Belt came to be seen, it was the end of salmon migration (Chida 2015: 150).

Final remarks

It has been often said that Japanese star lore has comparatively poorly developed, but this argument is insufficient. Such an argument has partially resulted from a lack of awareness among researchers (e.g., Renshaw and Ihara 1998, 2000). Although this short chapter has focused on only a few conspicuous constellations, it has shown the possibility to further explore a rich tradition of star lore in daily activities among the people of the archipelago. Since many cultural activities using planetariums are active in Japan, cultural astronomy will be a promising field to be pursued by researchers and citizens.

References

Arichi, Meri
    2006   Seven stars of Heaven and seven shrines on Earth: the Big Dipper and the Hie Shrine in the Medieval Period. *Culture and Cosmos* 10(1/2): 195–216.

Chida, Moriyasu 千田守康
    2015   *Stars of Homeland and a Japanese Glossary of Seasonal Stars.* 『ふるさとの星、和名歳時記』Sendai: Kahoku Shinpo.

Dolche, Lucia
    2006   The worship of celestial bodies in Japan: politics, rituals and icons. *Culture and Cosmos* 10(1 and 2): 3–43.

Goto, Akira 後藤 明
    1991   Fishing lore around Sendai Bay and Sanriku Coast. 「仙台湾 三陸の漁撈 民俗 In: Y. Amino, T. Ohbayashi, K. Tanigawa, N. Miyata and K. Mori (eds.), *The Sea and the Culture of Japanese Archipelago* 『海と列島文化』, Vol. 7, pp. 601–629. Tokyo: Shogakukan.
    2011   Archaeoastronomy and ethnoastronomy in the Ryukyu Islands: a preliminary report. In: C. Ruggles (ed.), *Archaeastronomy and Ethnoastronomy: Building Bridges between Cultures*, pp. 315–324. Cambridge: Cambridge University Press.

Kanezashi, Shozo 金指正三
    1974   *Horoscope and Star Ceremonies.* 『星占い 星祭り』Tokyo: Seiabo.

Katsumata, Takashi 勝俣隆
    2000   *Japanese Mythology Interpreted by Stars.* 『星座で読み解く日本神話』Tokyo: Taishukan.

Kitao, Kouichi 北尾浩一
    2001   *Living with Stars: An Attempt of Astronomical Folklore.* 『星と生きる： 天文 民俗学の試み』Kyoto: Win Kamogawa.
    2018   *Encyclopedia of Japanese Star Names.* 『日本の星名前事典』Tokyo: Harashobo.

Kuwahara, Shoji 桑原昭二
    1963   *A Collection of Japanese Star Names: Setouchi Inland Sea and Harima Country.* 『星の和名伝説集—瀬戸内はりまの星』 Osaka: Rokugatsusha.

Nojiri, Hoei 野尻抱影
    1958   *An Itinerancy of Constellations.* 『星座遍歴』Tokyo: Koseisha.
    1973   *A Dictionary of Japanese Star Names.* 『日本星名辞典』Tokyo: Chuokoron-sha.

Renshaw, Steven L. and Saori Ihara
- 1998 Astronomy in Japan: a cultural history. In: H. Selin (ed.), *Encyclopedia of the History of Science, Technology and Medicine in Non-Western Cultures*, pp. 342–354. New York: Kluwer Academic.
- 2000 A cultural history of astronomy in Japan. In: H. Selin (ed.), *Astronomy across Cultures: the History of Non-Western Astronomy*, pp. 385–407. New York: Kluwer Academic.

Sueoka, Tomio 末岡外美男
- 1979 *Stars of Ainu*. 『アイヌの星』 Asahikawa: Asahikawa-shosho. (In Japanese)

Uchida, Takeshi 内田武志
- 1973 *Dialects and Folklore of Stars*. 『星の方言と民俗』 Tokyo: Iwasaki bijutsusha.

Yanagita, Kunio and Ichiro Kurata 柳田国男・倉田一郎
- 1938 *Classified Glossary of Fishing Village*. 『分類漁村語彙』 Tokyo: Minkandenshono Kai.

2 Stars in mythology and classical literature

Stars in ancient mythology

The most ancient collections of Japanese myths exist in the *Kojiki* 『古事記』 *Records of Ancient Matters* (Chamberlain 1981; Heldt 2014) and the *Nishonshoki* 『日本書紀』 or *Nihongi* 『日本紀』 *Japanese Chronicles* (Aston 1972) compiled during the Yamato Dynasty 大和朝廷 during the eighth century. The Yamato Dynasty was based on an alliance of influential clans and the *Kojiki* records the history of the clan that had probably been produced by descendants of the emperor. On the other hand, the *Nihonshoki* was more influenced by Chinese philosophy, included myths from several clans, and often mentions different versions of the same mythological motif.

Many Japanese scholars now think that the *Kojiki* and *Nihonshoki* should be read as independent texts (Konoshi 1999; Ooms 2009: 29) and readers should be conscious of which text mythological stories below come from.

In ancient Japanese myths, surprisingly few references are been made to constellations. The principle god, Amaterasu-Omikami (hereafter Amaterasu) 天照大御神 (Heaven-Shining-Great-August-Deity) symbolizes the sun and her brother Tsukuyomi-no-mikoto 月読命 (Moon-Night-Possessor) symbolizes the moon. Neither of them, however, behaves as a constellation. Finally, their youngest brother, Takehaya Suwanowo-no-mikoto (hereafter Suwanowo) 建速須佐之男命 (His Brave-Swift-Impetuous-Male-Augustness), is often said to be a trickster and symbolized a "storm."

The most famous motif considered to be astronomical is Amaterasu's hiding in a rock-dwelling. Scared of her brother, Susanowo's violence at Takamaga-hara 高天原 (Plain of High Heaven), she escaped into the cave. According to the *Kojiki*:

> So thereupon the Heaven-Shining-Great-August-Deity, terrified at the sight, closed [behind her] the door of the Heavenly Rock-Dwelling*,

made it fast, and retired. Then the whole Plain of High Heaven* was obscured and all the Central Land of Reed Plains darkened. Owing to this, eternal night prevailed.
> (Chamberlain 1981: 64–65). * [Heavenly Rock-Dwelling: 天の岩屋戸; Central Land of Reed Plains: 葦原中国]

This story was believed to be about a solar eclipse and it belongs to a version of a mythological motif of the "hidden sun" (e.g., Chamberlain 1981). In order to discuss how to recover the light, myriad deities assemble in the bed of the Tranquil River of Heaven 天安河原. After several attempts to lure Amaterasu out the cave, Ameno-uzumeno-mikoto (hereafter Amenouzume) 天宇受売命 (Her Augustness Heavenly-Alarming-Female) danced, "pulling out the nipples of her breasts, pushing down her skirt-string usque ad privates partes" (Chamberlain 1981: 69). All the assembled deities laughed at this scene and Amaterasu slightly opened the door out of curiosity. Finally, she was pulled out of the cave and both the Plain of High Heaven and the Central Land of Reed n Plains again recovered light.

Primordial pair: Izanaki and Izanami

At the beginning of Japanese ancient mythology, seven generations of deities with abstract names emerged from primordial chaos and a brother and sister deities were born: Izanaki-no-mikoto (hereafter Izanaki) 伊邪那岐命 *Records of Ancient Matters* (Male-Who-Invites) and Izanami-no-mikoto (hereafter Izanami) 伊邪那美命 (Female-Who-Invites). In their names, *iza* probably means "to invite," *naki* means "calm sea" and *nami* means "wave."

Then, all the heavenly deities commanded these brother-sister deities "make, to consolidate and give birth to this drifting land"
So, the two gods

> standing upon the Floating Bridge of Heaven*, pushed down the jewelled spar and stirred with it, whereupon, when they had stirred the brine till it went curdle-curdle, and drew [the spear] up, the brine that dripped down from the end of the spear was piled up and became an island. This is the Island of Onogoro. [sic]
> (Chamberlain 1981: 21–22). * [Floating Bridge of Heaven: 天の浮橋]

Descending over this island, a pair of gods decided to mate. Izanaki proposed "well, then, let us walk around this mighty pillar of heaven and then join in bed ... you circle from the right to meet me, I will circle from the left to meet you" (Heldt 2014: 9). When they met after circulating the pillar of heaven, the goddess said, "What a fine boy!" Then the other god said, "What a fine girl!" (ibid.) They then mated, but their attempt ended in failure and the goddess delivered a limbless Leech Child (蛭子) who was sent away to the sea in a reed boat.

Chamberlain (1981: 24), as well as Heldt (2014: 10), in translating *Kojiki*, and Aston (1972: 16–17) in translating *Nihonshoki* all emphasized that the reason of the failure of the first attempt at mating was that the goddess sent a love call before the male god did; custom has it that man should have made a love call first. In the second trial, the male god sent a love call first after circling the pillar, and this time mating was successful.

Both Chamberlain (1981: 22) and Heldt (2014: 10) noted that the second attempt proceeded the same. But some Japanese scholars noticed that the direction of circling in the second trial was opposite to the first trial: the god circled from right to left and the goddess from left to right as noted in one book of *Nihonshoki* (Katsumata 2000: 73–74).

The custom in which boys and girls circle around the pole in opposite directions and meet is often reported from minority groups in southwestern China and this custom is a part of the festival called *utagaki* 歌垣, a gathering of men and women who sang courtship songs to each other and danced. One of its purposes was to find a spouse. This custom was recorded in a *Fudoki* work, *Hitachi no kuni fudoki*『常陸国風土記』(Hitachi is in present Ibaraki Prefecture) (Aoki 1997: 41).

Why should the man circle from the right and the woman from the left? This probably came from the Chinese philosophical belief that heaven turns from right to left and that the earth turns from left to right. Also, there is a belief that man should turn to the left and that the women should turn to the right (Katsumata 2000: 76–77).

When we look up at the heavenly north from the latitude of China or Japan, heaven is seen to be circulating from right to left. Comparatively, the earth appeared to be circulating from left to right. This is said to be the proper rule of heaven (male, Izanaki) and earth (female, Izanami). In addition, *Ameno-Mihashira* 天の御柱 around which Izanaki and Izanami moved around, translates as "a pillar in the middle of heaven." This might be the heavenly north.

Among deities with abstract names who appeared before Izanaki and Izanami, the first-born was Ameno-minkanushi-no-kami 天之御中主神, whose name is translated as "Master-of-the-August-Center of Heaven" (Chamberlain 1981: 15) or "Master-Mighty Center of Heaven" (Heldt 2014: 7). It is arguable whether this deity was Polaris since the Heavenly

Arctic at this time did not correspond to Polaris today. However, this thought must have come from Chinese philosophy. After the introduction of Esoteric Buddhism, this deity came to be associated with Moyken 妙見, which symbolized Polaris (more discussed in Chapter 6).

Three young noble men and Orion's Belt

Goddess Izanami then delivered the Japanese islands and a series of gods. When she delivered Hinokagutsuichi-no-kami 火之迦具土神, the fire god, she died because her genitals were burned by the fire from her offspring. Her husband, Izanami, went to the realm of the dead to see his wife. However, since seeing her body already rotten, he flew away to the realm of the living. He purified his body in the sea when he came back from hell where he met his dead wife (and also sister) Izanami.

Then, in the water, three Tsutsunowo-Sanshin 筒男三神, three-brother gods of Tsutsunowo were born. There is an opinion that *tsutsu* meant "a star": *tsutsu* literally means "tube" or "hole" in heaven and refers to stars. In the oldest collection of poems, the *Manyoshu* 『万葉集』 (compiled from the late seventh century to the eighth century), there is a term *yu-tsutsu* 夕筒, meaning an evening star (*yu* means "evening"). But Motoori Norinaga 本居宣長 (1730–1801), a famous Japanese classical scholar 国学者, was critical of the opinion that *tsutsu* refers to a star. He argued that *tsutsu* came from a place name, Tsutsu on Tsusima Island 対馬, which lies between Kyushu and the Korean Peninsula (Kanezashi 1974: 6).

Setting aside etymological questions, the three brothers were named Soko-Tsutsunowo-no-mikoto (Bottom Tsutsunowo-no-mikoto) 底筒之男命, Naka-Tsutsunowo-no-mikoto (Middle Tsutsunowo-no-mikoto) 中筒之男命, Uwa-Tsutsunowo-no-mikoto (Surface Tsutsunowo-no-mikoto) 上筒之男命. These three brothers were the main gods worshiped by maritime groups of the Sumiyoshi Clan. The combination of the bottom, middle, and surface of the water may symbolize the three stars of Orion's Belt that appear one after another vertically on the horizon (Nojiri 1955: 18–20; Katsumata 2000: 102–124).

In both the *Kojiki* and the *Nihonshoki*, another three brothers were born at the same time: Sokotsu-owatatsumi-no-kami 底津綿津見神 (bottom), Nakatsu-owatatsumi-no-kami 中津綿津見神 (middle), and Uwa-tsu-owatatsumi-no-kami 上津綿津見神 (surface). Here, "*watatsumi*" is the name of a sea god and these three brothers are major gods worshiped by the maritime Azumi Clan (Chamberlain 1981: 49–50). However, I will focus on Tsutsunowo-sanshin below.

I argue that Orion was an important navigational constellation in ancient Japan, in particular, when navigating the west–east direction in the

Setouchi Inland Sea. The Sumiyoshi Shrine 住吉神社, where the three gods are worshiped, is located on the seaside in southern Osaka at the eastern end of the Inland Sea. At the Sumiyoshi Shrine, the major temple was constructed mainly for praying for safety on the sea and the three shrines that are dedicated to each deity are aligned in a straight line with the impression that they symbolize the three stars of Orion's Belt (Figure 2.1).

The August descent from Heaven 天孫降臨

After the birth of the three brothers, Tsutsunowo-Sanshin, three high-status deities (mentioned at the beginning of this section) were born: when Izanami washed his left eye, Amaterasu was born; when he washed his right eye, Tsukuyomi was born; and when he washed his nose, Suwanowo was born. They occupied the highest positions among deities in heaven, a position called *Amatsukami* 天津神.

Amaterasu delegated heavenly deities to earth in order to govern the underworld, but they were amused by the deities on earth, *Kunitsukami* 国津神. Finally, Amaterasu sent her grandson, Ninigi-no-Mikoto (hereafter Ninigi) 瓊瓊杵尊 (His Augustness Prince-Rice-ear-Ruddy-Plenty) to earth:

> When he [Ninigi] was about to descend, one, who had been sent in advance to clear the way, returned and said: "There is one god who

Figure 2.1 Sumiyoshi Shrine 住吉神社 in Osaka.

dwells at the eight-cross-roads of Heaven*, the length of whose nose is seven hands, and the length of whose back is more than seven fathoms. Moreover, a light shines from his mouth and from his posteriors. His eye-balls are like an eight-hand mirror and have a ruddy glow like the Akakagachi [sic].

(Aston 1972: 77). * [Ama-no-yachimata 天の八街]

That god was Sarutahiko-no-Ohkami (hereafter Sarutahiko) 猿田彦大神. Ninigi wanted to send a god to inquire into the Sarutahiko closing the eight-cross roads of heaven, but most of them were afraid of the Sarutahiko. He has red eyes like *Akakagachi*, a kind of red ground cherry (*hozuki*).

Finally, Ninigi commanded Amenouzume by saying:

> Thou art superior to others in the power of thy looks. Thou hadst better go and question him ... So Amenozume forthwith bared her breasts and, pushing down the band of her garment below her navel, confronted him with a mocking laugh.
>
> (Aston 1972: 77)

Then, Sarutahiko said that he was waiting there to welcome high-status gods from heaven and lead them to the "Reed-Plain-1500-Autumns-Fair-Rice-Land" 豊葦原の千秋長五百秋の水穂国. Amenouzume was a goddess who lured Amaterasu outside with a sexual dance when Amaterasu was hiding in the Rock Cave of Heaven (Amano Iwato Cave). In a similar way, the Amenouzume could accomplish her duty again by using her sexual charms.

Katsumata Takashi argued that the eight crossroads of heaven correspond to the Pleiades, since there are many ethnographic examples in which the Pleiades was analogous to many holes or sieves in heaven. In addition, Aldebaran corresponds to the red eye of Sarutahiko and the V-shape of the Hyades corresponds to his long nose. Then Orion is Amenouzume who is dancing: Orion's Belt corresponds to her belt and Orion's Blade pushed down the band of her garment (Katsumata 2000: 180–184) (Figure 2.2).

God that symbolized a star

When Ninigi and his follower gods descended to the "Reed-Plain-1500-Autumns-Fair-Rice-Land" stated above, one writing in the *Nihonshoki* explains: The heavenly deity sent Futsunushi-no-kami 経津主神 and Take-mika-tsuchi-no-kami 武甕槌神 to tranquilize the Central Land of Reed-Plains. Now these two gods said that in heaven there is an evil deity called Amatsu-mikahoshi 天津甕星, or Ameno-kagasewo 天之香香背男,

Figure 2.2 Constellations supposed to correspond to the myth of "The August Descent from Heaven" (Katsumata 2000, frontispiece).
Source: courtesy of Katsumata Takashi.

who shine and are noisy like flies. At the same time, grass and trees also speak loudly (Katsumata 2000: 46). Most of the earthly gods finally surrendered to heavenly gods, but only Ama (heaven)-tsu (of)-mika (big round object)-hoshi (star) never surrendered.

The meaning of Amatsu-mikahoshi has not been determined definitively, but *mika* probably means "a big round object" and could indicate a big star. Researchers have attempted to identify which star corresponds to it: Venus, Mars, Sirius, Canopus, a comet, a meteor, or something else. Setting aside the problem of identification, most researchers agree that the Amatsu-mikahoshi symbolized local chiefs who did not surrender to the Yamato Dynasty. There are quite a few shrines where Amatsu-mikahoshi is worshiped as a principle god from Kyushu to the northern Kanto region (north of Tokyo) and it seems that these shrines originated in the unification of local powers by the Yamato Dynasty (Katsumata 2000: 46–64).

Urashima and the Pleiades

The oldest surviving literature after the *Kojiki* and the *Nihonshoki* is the *Fudoki* 『風土記』, which is a description of the regional climate, culture, and geography collected from local countries during the eighth century. In the *Tangono-kuni Fudoki Itsubun* 『丹後国風土記逸文』, a partially lost work from Tango Country (north of Kyoto), there is a story of "Urashima Taro" 浦島太郎, which has been a popular folktale in Japan (Chamberlain 1892). The origin of this story can be traced back to the *Tangono-kuni Fudoki Itsubun* and its content is rather different from the Urashima Taro story told more recently. What follows is a summary of the original story.

The *Tangono-kuni Fudoki Itsubun* explains: An ancestor of the local chief, Urano-shimako 浦嶋子 (hereafter, Shimako) was fishing on the sea and found a rainbow-colored turtle. He brought the turtle into the boat, but it turned into a beautiful lady. She invited him to the island that lies far beyond the sea. At the entrance, Shimako met seven children and these seven children were called *subaru* (the Pleiades.) Then he met an eighth child, who was called *amefuri*, which means "raining" in Japanese. This term came from one of the 28 *Sei Shuku* (28 houses in Chinese zodiac system), and corresponds to 8 stars of the Hyades in the Taurus (Kanezashi 1974: 12).

Shimako had enjoyed his time with the lady for three years, but he felt homesick and wanted to go back to his country. The lady handed him a decorated magical box, *tamakushige*, and told him to never open the box. He thought that only three days had passed, but in his world, 300 years had passed already. The people in his country thought that Shimako was lost forever and he was only a legend. Being nostalgic for the lady, he opened the box that he was prohibited to open. Suddenly, smoke rose and Shimako quickly aged and died.

This story is one of the oldest mentions of the Pleiades or any constellation in Japanese classical literature. However, even in the older version of the Urashima Taro story found in the *Nihonshoki* (Aston 1972: 368) and the *Manyoshu* 万葉集, no mention was made of stars.

On the other hand, the name of the Pleiades is mentioned in *Makura-no-sohi* 『枕草子』, the famous essay written by a woman officer in the tenth century. In this essay, *subaru* (the Pleiades) is mentioned together with other stars, such as *hikoboshi* 彦星 (Altair), *myoujou* 明星 (Venus or morning star), *yutsutsu* 夕星 (evening star), and *yobai-boshi* (night crawling star, shooting star).

The moon in classical literature, the *Manyoshu*, and elsewhere

The *Manyoshu* is the oldest anthology of traditional Japanese poems and was compiled during the late eighth century. Most poems are in a short form called *tanka* 短歌, which consist of the Japanese syllable pattern of 5–7–5–7–7. There are also longer poems called *choka* 長歌. *Choka* poems were often composed by court poets, but there are some others composed by anonymous people who were probably ordinary workers, such as farmers, soldiers, and others.

There are surprisingly few poems that mention stars. In contrast, there are many poems that are referring to the moon as a symbolic expression of love. There is an interesting example in which the moon is symbolized as a ship voyaging in the starry night:

> Behold, the waves of clouds are seen
> Upon the sea of heaven, and
> The moon, as a ship, goes sailing
> Amid innumerable stars.
>
> (No. 1068; Honda 1967: 93)

This poem was composed by a famous court poet, Kakinomotono Hitomaro 柿本人麻呂. He also composed:

> Rowing the bright Moon's boat, its man goes there
> over heaven's seas so calm, so for.
>
> (No. 3611; Honda 1967: 266)

There is another poem composed by an anonymous writer:

> In the sea of heaven
> I see the lone man row
> The lunar boat so bright
> With *katsura* oars tonight.
>
> (No. 2223; Honda 1967: 178)

Here, *katsura* is a plant, *Cercidiphyllum japonicum*, and the Japanese commonly believed that *katsura* trees grew on the moon. A similar idea is found in the *Tosa Nikki* 『土佐日記』, a diary written by Kino Tsurayuki 紀貫之 in the early tenth century, when he was returning from Tosa County (Kochi Prefecture) to Kyoto by boat. He composed one short poem that sees the moon as a boat on the sea:

> The oar strikes through the moon on the waves;
> The boat presses against the sky in the sea.

Following this poem, there was another one in which a *katsura* tree is mentioned together with the moon. Helen McClullough translates *katsura* as "cinnamon tree":

> A cinnamon tree!/Surely it is no other/Catching the oar
> Of the boat rowing over/The moon in the watery depth
> (McCullough 1985: 275)

The sun and ancient capital design

The Asuka Period (592–710), when the *Manyoshu* was compiled, corresponds to the latter half of the mythical age of the *Kojiki* and the *Nihonshoki*. The capital of Asuka was north of the Nara Heijo-kyo Capital 平城京, which is the foundation of the Japanese Dynasty that was founded in 710.

In the Asuka Period, Emperor Tenmu 天武天皇 was particularly proficient in astronomy (Aston 1972, Vol. 2: 301; Saito 1982). In the Tenmu Era (673–686), Emperor Tenmu had founded a professional system of astronomical observation and a calendar system that were both introduced from China. A platform was for the first time erected from which to do horoscopes by means of the stars (Aston 1972, Vol. 2: 326). In China, the fundamental axis for city planning is the north-south line and the Polaris or Arctic north at that age held a primary importance. Therefore, the north-south line was called warp 経 and the east-west line was called weft 緯.

Certainly, the north-south line was recognized as an important axis, as seen from Nakatsu-michi 中ツ道 (middle road) and Shimotsu-michi 下ツ道 (lower road), which runs from north to south along the eastern and western border of the capital (Aston 1972, Vol. 2: 319).

Although there is controversy surrounding the existence of Emperor Seimu 成務, the thirteenth Emperor belonging to the Mythological Age, the *Nihonshoki* describes Emperor Seimu as follows:

> In this way East and West were reckoned as in a line with the sun, while North and South were reckoned as athwart the sun. The sunny side of the mountains was called the 'light-face' and shady side of the mountains the "back-face" [sic].
> (Aston 1972: 216)

Here, "a line with the sun" is a translation of "sun's warp" and "athwart the sun" is a translation of the "sun's weft."

However, one long poem found in the *Manyoshu* states that:

> When the Emperor moved to the palace new
> in Fujiwara Town,
> and looked around him,
> standing on the shore of Lake Haniyasu,
> he saw Mt. Kagu in the east
> all clad with vernal green,
> fair Mt. Unebi in the west,
> and Miminashi soaring in the north,
> and crystal water welling in the palace grounds
>
> (Anonymous No. 52; Honda 1967: 7)

This poem is admiring the new capital of Fujiwara-kyo 藤原京, which was planned by Tenmu and founded by Emperor Jito 持統天皇. She was a wife of Emperor Tenmu and became empress after the death of Emperor Tenmu. The capital of Fujiwara was established in the northwestern part of Asuka, during the Jito Era (690–698) (Ooms 2009: 76). In the above poem, Mt. Kagu 香具山 is said to be the "sun's warp" and Mt. Unebi 畝傍山 is said to be the "sun's weft." Therefore, in this poem, the east represents the warp and the west the weft. We are not sure whether the sun's warp meant the east-west line and sun's weft the north–south line, as written in the *Nihonshoki*, or whether warp meant the east and weft the west. However, it is certain that the east-west line is as important as, or more important than, the north-south line in the Asuka Period (Arakawa 2001: 64–69) (Figure 2.3).

North as the principle orientation

After this period, the capital was moved to Nara (Heijo-kyo Capital 平城京) in 710, then to Nagaoka (Nagaoka-kyo Capital 長岡京) in 784, and finally to Kyoto (Heian-kyo Capital 平安京) in 794. These new capitals had been planned following the north–south line as a primary axis. In Kyoto, the north came to be conceived by the ordinary people as "upper" or *kami* 上, and the south is conceived as "lower" or *shimo* 下. This concept continues to be used until today: going north is expressed as "*agaru*" 上がる (going up) and going south as "*sagaru*" 下がる (going down).

At the beginning of Heian-kyo at the end of the eighth century, Daigokuden 大極殿 (the Imperial Palace) was located in the middle of the northern border of the capital and this location is different from the Imperial Palace location today. The Jishu Jinja 地主神社 (Land God Shrine)

Stars in mythology and literature 35

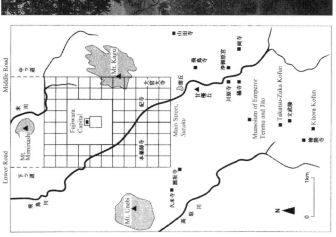

Figure 2.3 Fujiwara Kyo capital and surrounding mountains.

Notes
a Plan of Fujiwara Capital (modified from Arakawa 2001, Figure 25; courtesy of Arakawa Hiroshi).
b Mt. Unebi seen from the summit of Amano-Kagu-yama ("Heavenly Mt. Kagu").

36 *Stars in mythology and literature*

located north-west of the Imperial Palace and it is said that the emperor worshiped the Polaris that could be seen behind this shrine.

Kitano Tenmangu 北野天満宮, located where Jishu Jinja was originally positioned, is said to be designed so that the Polar Star shines behind the main architectural axis. Kitano Tenmangu is a shrine where the soul of the famous scholar Sugawara Michizane 菅原道真 was enshrined. Sugawara Michizane was expelled from Kyoto and sent to Kyushu for political reasons and died there. Many strange phenomena followed his death, such as the appearance of a big meteorite, thunder, and other occurrences. He later came to be called Tenjin 天神, which means "heavenly god." Tenjin is originally associated with the god of thunder and this thought, in turn, came to be syncretized with the worship of Polaris.

Before the main shrine, there was situated a gate called the Sankou-Mon Gate 三光門 (Figure 2.4a), which means "three lights gate," representing the sun, the moon and the star (Polaris).

On the gate, symbols of the sun (Figure 2.4b), the crescent moon (Figure 2.4c), and the full moon (Figure 2.4d) are expressed, but the symbol of Polaris is lacking. The main shrine and the gate are facing

Figure 2.4 Kitano Tenmangu Shrine and "Three Lights Gate".

Notes
a Three Lights Gate facing almost true south.
b Symbol of the sun.
c Symbol of the crescent moon.
d Symbol of the full moon.

almost true south and the people prayed to the shrine are facing true north, toward Polaris. This is the reason why the symbol of Polaris is not expressed on this gate.

References

Aoki, Michiko Y.
    1997   *Records of Wind and Earth: A Translation of Fudoki with Introduction and Commentaries.* Monographs of the Association of Asian Studies.

Arakawa, Hiroshi 荒川紘
    2001   *The Cosmology of the Japanese: From the Asuka Period to the Present Age.* 『日本人の宇宙観: 飛鳥時代から現代まで』 Tokyo: Kinokuniya-shoten.

Aston W.G.
    1972   *Nihongi: Chronicle of Japan from the Earliest Times to A.D. 697.* Tokyo: Tuttle.

Chamberlain, Basil Hall
    1892   *Urashima, The Fisher Boy.* Tokyo: Kobunsha.
    1981   *The Kojiki: Records of Ancient Matters.* Tokyo: Tuttle. (Originally published in 1906).

Heldt, Gustav
    2014   *Kojiki: An Account of Ancient Matters.* New York: Columbia University Press.

Honda, H.H.
    1967   *The Manyoshu: A New and Complete Translation.* Tokyo: The Hokuseido.

Konoshi, Takamitsu 神野志隆光
    1999   *Kojiki and Nihonshoki.* 『古事記と日本書紀』 Tokyo: Kodansha.

Kanezashi, Shozo 金指正三
    1974   *Horoscope and Star Festival.* 『星占い星祭り』 Tokyo: Seiabo.

Katsumata, Takashi 勝俣隆
    2000   *Japanese Mythology Interpreted by Constellation.* 『星座で読み解く日本神話』 Tokyo: Taishukan.

McCullough, Helen C.
    1985   *Kokin Wakashū: The First Imperial Anthology of Japanese Poetry.* Stanford: Stanford University Press.

Nojiri, Hoei 野尻抱影
    1955   *Collection of myths and legends of stars.* 『星の神話・傳説集成』 Tokyo: Koseisha.

Ooms, Herman
    2009   *Imperial Politics and Symbolism in Ancient Japan: The Tenmu Dynasty, 650–800.* Honolulu: University of Hawai'i Press.

Saito, Kuniji 斉藤国治
    1982   *The Astronomy of the Asuka Period.* 『飛鳥時代の天文学』 Tokyo: Kawade-shobo.

3 Star lore of the Hokkaido Ainu

Hokkaido Ainu

Japan's northernmost island, Hokkaido, is a unique area where rice cultivation was impossible until modern times. Hokkaido is the homeland of indigenous hunter–gatherers known as the Ainu (Figure 3.1a). Historically, the Ainu have also lived in Southern Sakhalin and the Kuril Islands. In a remote past, the Ainu people probably lived in northern Honshu as well.

Five or six local Ainu groups have been identified within Hokkaido, but according to the Hokkaido Ainu Culture Center (now located in the Hokkaido Museum), the dialects of the Hokkaido Ainu are grouped into Southwestern Groups and Northeastern Groups (Figure 3.1b). The latter demonstrates some similarities with the groups of Sakhalin and the Kuril Islands. As will be shown below, this division well accords with the regional differences in housing orientation and burials.

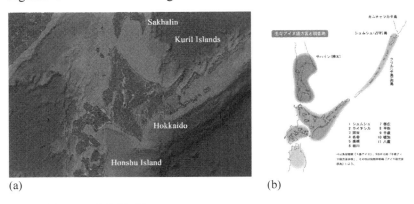

Figure 3.1 Map of Hokkaido.

Notes
a Map of Hokkaido and other islands.
b Deialect of Ainu Language (http://ainugo.hm.pref.hokkaido.lg.jp/html/01_01_02_01_00.html).

The Ainu were never an isolated people. On the contrary, they actively traded with the Japanese and with groups on the northeastern part of the Asian continent. Thus, their possessions consist of items both from Japan (e.g., samurai swords, kimonos, etc.) and Asia (e.g., glass beads, metal artifacts, etc.).

The Hokkaido Ainu's economy largely consisted of foraging, although they also practiced small-scale farming of millet. Their most important staple food was salmon and the Ainu people traditionally caught several species of salmon and trout between spring and fall. Then they preserved salmon meat by smoking it and also hunted deer, wild pig, rabbit and bear, which all comprised important components of the Ainu diet (Watanabe 1972).

Today, the Ainu people typically live a modern lifestyle, using automobiles, mobile phones, electricity, and other modern technologies. But a cultural revival movement has recently begun. For instance, a ceremony called *icharupa* has been held annually on the day close to the summer solstice in Shibetsu Town in eastern Hokkaido (Goto 2018). The purpose of this ceremony is to console the souls of the Ainu fighters killed during the Kunashiri-Menashi war against the Japanese and opposing Ainu groups in 1789.

Planets

There are various vernacular names for the sun and the moon. The sun is widely called *cupkamuy*, "star of god" (*cup* [constellation], *kamuy* [god]) or *tokapcupkamuy*, "bright star" (*tokap* [bright]). In contrast, the moon is called *kunnecupkamuy*, "dark star" (*kunne* [dark]) or *ancupkamuy*, "night star" (*an* [night]).

There are also various vernacular names for planets. In general, planets were called *raykurnociw*, "star of death's spirit" (*ray* [death], *kur* [spirit], *nociw* [star]), or *sitturaynukur*, "wandering people" (*sitturaynu* [wander], *kur* [people]). In particular, Venus is called *nisatsawotonociw* (*nisat* [dawn], *sawot* [to escape], star), which means "morning star" (Suoeka 2009).

There is fragmentary ethnographic information suggesting that the Ainu worshiped Venus for ritual reasons (Hatanaka 1971: 105) and that they prayed to Venus on a daily basis (Hokkaido Board of Education 1987: 50). Sueoka Tomio, whose data and observations have provided some of the most important resources for studying Ainu star lore, pointed out that when some Ainu groups set up an *inaw* (sacred stripped branch used for Ainu rituals) on a *nusa* (alter) (Figure 3.2), they placed the *inaw* facing Venus and that they directed the head of the dead toward the morning star (i.e., eastward) (Sueoka 2009: 109). Some Ainu used Venus, along with Polaris and Ursa Minor, as navigation stars (Yoshida 1952: 124).

Figure 3.2 Sacred Altar dedicated by *inaw*.
Source: courtesy of Shibetsu Town Board of Education.

The Ainu had an interesting legend concerning Venus and Mercury:

> One day, *pakorkamuy* (*pakor* [pemphigus], *kamuy* [god]) came to Ainu villages and many Ainu suffered from pemphigus. Every time someone killed *pakorkamuy*, he resurrected with stronger evil powers. The people debated and decided to send the most beautiful star, *nisatsawotnociw* (morning star), to marry him. When she married *pakorkamuy*, he was tamed and severe diseases disappeared from this world. Then *nisatsawotnociw* came to rise with a daughter, *poturannociw*, (*po* [child], *tura* [to bring together, *kamuy* [star]), Mercury, in the dawn sky.
>
> (Sueoka 2009: 109–110)

This story is interesting since Mercury is said to be a daughter of Venus. Another legend has it that the morning star and evening star were sisters. Both of them were very beautiful and the elder sister morning star winked at *pakorkamuy*. At that moment, the morning star conceived and delivered a beautiful daughter, *ponociw* "child star," Mercury (*pon* [samll], *nociw* [star]).

There is another belief that Mercury was an egg of a Blakiston's fish owl that was raised by sunlight. If Mercury was seen beside *kamuymarapto* (Venus), it was thought that fishing would be successful that year

(Sueoka 2009: 110). In the Chitose River Basin in southwest Hokkaido, Venus was called *marapto* (bear head) or *kauymarapto* (bear god's head).

Stars in spring

The Big Dipper and Ursa Major

Ursa Major, including the Big Dipper, is the most widely known constellation among the Ainu. Taking this constellation as an example, I will show regional variation in vernacular names and beliefs behind them among the Ainu.

The Big Dipper was called *cinukarkur*, "the star-gods we see" (*ci* [we], *nukar* [to see], *kur* [demigod]) throughout Hokkaido. In the eastern region, there is another name for the Big Dipper, *mosirnoka-nociw*, "star shape-like a human country" (*mosir* [human world], *noka* [shape of], star) (Sueoka 1979: 32–44).

The Ainu saw the five stars of Big Dipper, from Phecda (γ) to Alkaid (η), as the shape of a boat, *cipnokanociw*, which means "boat-shaped star" (*cip* [a boat], shape, star). This name is found in both the eastern and southern (Toshima Peninsular) regions (Sueoka 1979: 40). This is a similar view to those of the fishermen in the main islands of Japan. Probably the Ainu used this star as an index of longline fishing season (spring) (Sueoka 1979: 39–42). Some people said that the seven stars of Urso Minor were the fish caught with this longline. Also, Polaris was a big fish and the fishing boat turning around it is Ursa Minor (Sueoka 2009: 210).

The same star line (γ to η) is called *kunociw*, "bow star" (*ku* [bow]), from central to eastern Hokkaido. Among these groups, the people of the Tokachi region in particular retained a name *aynociw* for α and β, which means "arrow star" (*ay* [arrow]) (Sueoka 1979: 19–20).

In Hokkaido, where the Big Dipper becomes a circumpolar star, the circulation of the Big Dipper was seen to be dancing women, called, *upopoketa*. *Upopo* is the name of a dance and *keta* means "star," and this name is found mainly in the northern region (Sueoka 1979: 32). A similar name, *upopo-nociw*, is used in the center region of Hokkaido (Sueoka 1979: 35). In a similar way, the Big Dipper is called *kuttokonoka-nociw*, "stars like a god lying with face up" (*kuttoko* [lying face up], *noka* [shape of], star) in central–eastern and southern Hokkaido. It is also called *upsinoka-nociw*, "stars (like a god) lying with face down" (*upsi* [lying face down]).

In the central region, the Big Dipper is also called *iwanpon-nociw*, "six stars" (*iwan* [six], *pon* [small], *nociw* [star]). In the south–southwestern region (from the Chitose Basin to the Hidaka Area), the Big Dipper is called *arwanpon-nociw*, "seven small stars" (*arwan* [seven], small, stars).

Only on the Toshima Peninsula region is the Big Dipper also called *wakkakup-nociw*, literally meaning "dipper" (*wakka* [water], *ku* [tool], *pu* [to drink], star) (Sueoka 1979: 73).

To the Ainu, the bear is a god with the highest status and many star legends depicted bears. The most famous one is about *samaennociw*, told widely except for in the south and southwestern regions:

> In the past, the bear who served as a god of Samaen got drunk and accidentally killed a dog that the god cared about. The bear stole a seedling of a halibut tree and planted it. The tree grew higher and higher and eventually reached heaven. The bear then climbed the tree and escaped to heaven. Samaen followed the bear climbing the tree and they fought for six days in heaven. Finally, Samaen himself became the star, the Big Dipper.
>
> (Sueoka 1979: 65–66)

There is another story concerning the Big Dipper and bears in the north and northeastern region: in the past, *siarasarus-kamuy-noka-nociw*, "bear with a long tail god star" (*si* [self], *ara* [side], *sar* [tail], *us* [bear], *noka* [shape], *nociw* [star]), was scared:

> Originally, the bear was a daughter of a chief in Sakhalin who married the chief in Soya Kotan, located in northern Hokkaido. Even after transforming into a bear, she was very gentle, saving distressed children and helping people hunt. One day, the chief (her husband) went into the forest. The bear, who missed her husband, rushed over him, but the chief was scared and tried to kill the bear with a poison arrow. At the moment when the chief shot the arrow, a heavenly god felt sorry for the bear and pulled up the bear to heaven. The bear became Ursa Major: the rise is her waist and the handle is her tail.
>
> (Sueoka 2009: 180–181)

Leo and Bootes

For the typical spring constellation Leo, the Ainu people gave a name, *inaw-ru-noka-nociw*, "*inaw* shaped star" (*inaw*, *ru* [hair style], *noka* [like], star). As mentioned, *inaw* is a religious object shaved from a willow branch (Figure 3.2), but in this case, the constellation appears to be of chiefs who put an *inaw* crown, *sapanpe*, on their heads during rituals (Figure 3.3). Legend has it that an Ainu chief was protesting against the severe employment imposed by the Japanese but that he was caught and to be executed. One night he succeeded in escaping the prison, went into the sea, and never returned. The legend also says that he ascended into heaven

Figure 3.3 Sapanpe (*inaw* crowns) exhibited in the Ainu Cultural Museum, Biratori.

and became this constellation. Other groups saw the curved line of Leo as a rorqual whale, calling it *aspe-kor-humpe* (*aspe* [something that stands up], *kor* [to have], *humpe* [whale]) (Siueoka 2009: 248–258).

For Bootes, which contains the red star Arcturus, the Ainu gave the name *hure-sumari* (red fox). In the past, *sumari* (a fox) stole a fish from

Samaen (a shaman as well as an otter), but the fox was caught by Samaen. The fox tried to free himself by promising to give his daughter to Samaen but escaped without fulfilling the promise. The fox mistakenly trampled the otter's face during the escape and that is why otter's face is flat. The angry otter sprinkled salmon eggs onto the fox's face, which is why his face (Arcturus) became red (Sueoka 2009: 294–295).

Stars in summer

Altair rises in the eastern horizon and often serves as a navigational star. On the Okhotsk Coast, there is a sad legend about Altair. During the Kunashiri-Menasi battle against the Japanese and hostile Ainu (1798), the Ainu groups from this area escaped to the Notsuke Peninsula, near Shibetsu Town. Seeing Altair rising from the east, behind Kunashiri Island, the people prayed to the star that they would be transported to the island. Thus, Altair came to be called *cikusakur*, "the guardian god for water transportation" (*cik* [we], *kusa* [transport by boat], *kur* [people or demigod]). The two small stars beside Altair were said to be the servants of *cikusakur* (Sueoka 2009: 400–402).

In a northern area like Hokkaido, Scorpio is only seen low above the horizon. The Ainu refer to Scorpio as *hoyaw* (dragon) or *horkaterkep* (crayfish).

Stars in autumn

After *panoka*, the Milky Way, sets in the autumn sky, there appears an M-shaped Cassiopeia in the middle of the sky. The Ainu saw Cassiopeia as related to fishing activities: one boat consists of α and β, and the other boats are γ and ε. γ is a *yas* (a net) that is pulled between two boats. The name of Cassiopeia, *yasyanoka-nociw*, means "boats that pull nets" (Sueoka 2009: 427).

Just as the Greeks saw Perseus as the appearance of a hero holding demon Gorgon's head, the Ainu saw the same stars as an appearance of a priestess who is praying to cure the diseased people with *inaw* and ritual items in her both hands; Pegasus is called *kinrakamuy* (*kinra* [maiden or priestess], god) (Sueoka 2009: 485).

The rectangular shape of Pegasus was considered by the Ainu to be a rectangular hole where winds came from. They called it *makwanohap*, which means "a vault." There is a legend concerning this constellation that says that one day a young Ainu told a god that he wanted to ascend to heaven to see his dead parents. The god refused at first, but he ultimately agreed, since the young Ainu begged repeatedly. The god tried to dig a hole around the Milky Way, but there were too many stars. The god then dug a hole where a space was formed and that is why Pegasus is located in its present location (Sueoka 2009: 444).

Stars in winter

The Pleiades

The main subsistence for the Ainu was hunting and gathering, but they also practiced small-scale farming of millet. When women were stepping on the grass dew of early spring in the field, they knew it was sowing season: they observed the heliacal rise of *toytanronociw*, the seasonal star for agriculture (*toyta* [gardening], *anro* [want to do], star). This name refers to the Pleiades, but strangely enough, the Pleiades is more often called *torannenociw*, which means "idle star that hates agriculture" (*toranne* [idle]). In relation to this name, legend has it that six stars of Pleiades were originally six or seven idle girls who ascended the heaven to avoid agriculture (Sueoka 2009: 231). This belief about the Pleiades is similar to that of native North Americans (Miller 1997).

Orion

The three stars of Orion's Belt are called *reneskur*, or "three people follow" (*ren* [three], *eus* [people to follow], *kur* [demigod]), and this name means that Orion's Belt rises, following *torannenociw*, idle stars (the Pleiades).

The whole constellation of Orion is called Siyapka, meaning "a great deer." Legend has it that Siyapka was a king of the forest. When Siyapka was leading a herd of dears in the forest, three skillful hunters approached from leeward to the herd and tried to shoot arrows. Siyapka sensed danger and went in front of the herd to let the other deer escape, but one arrow hit his belly. The other deer could escape but Siyapka died. The owl god in heaven was watching this scene and felt very sorry for Siyapka. The god let Siyapka into heaven and three stars of Orion's Belt showed the arrow that hit Siyapka (Suoeka 2009: 545–552).

Sirius

When Siyapka (Orion) rose high in the sky, Sirius appears in the eastern horizon. The Ainu in central and northern Hokkaido saw this star as a hunter who is pursuing a deer, which is why Sirius was called *kimunkurnociw* (*kimun* [to go to mountain], *kur* [demigod], star) (Sueoka 2009:

573). The Ainu used Sirius as a guiding star for orientation and time-reckoning when they were hunting in the forest (Sueoka 2009: 580).

Sirius rises at *cupko* (winter solstice sunrise point) during the cold winter and sets at *cuppoko* (winter solstice sunset point) at the end of March. In eastern Hokkaido, Sirius is called *rupumpe*, icicle (*rup* [ice], *un* [of], *pe* [water]) (Sueoka 2009: 578).

Gemini

In southwestern Hokkaido, Gemini is called *asrupenokanociw* (*as* [to stand], *rup* [head], *e* [ear], *noka* [shape], nociw [star]). The Ainu seem to see the pair star of Gemini as the right and left ears of a bear. When this constellation rises in the early evening slightly north of *cupketok* (summer solstice rising point), the sun started to come back from the winter solstice rising point to *cupkarantom* (equinox sun-rising point). When the Ainu saw that this constellation rises in the evening, they understood that the *iomante* (bear ceremony; see Chapter 7 for more information) season is near. When this constellation came to a zenith in the early evening of late March, snow began to melt, and salmon came up the rivers (Sueoka 2009: 527–528).

References

Goto, Akira 後藤　明
    2018   House and burial orientations of the Hokkaido Ainu, indigenous hunter-gatherers of northern Japan. *Meditarranean Archaeology and Archaeometry* 18(2): 173–180

Hatanaka, Takeo 畑中 武夫
    1971   *Beliefs of the Ainu.* 『アイヌの信仰』 Sappporo: Senjuminzoku Bunka Kyokai.

Hokkaido Kyoiku Iinkai [Hokkaido Board of Education] 北海道教育委員会
    1987   *Urgent Field Research on Ethnography of the Ainu, Vol. 6 (Tokachi & Abashiri).* 『アイヌ民俗文化財調査報告書』 6巻：十勝 網走地方 Sappopro: Hokkaido Government Office.

Miller, Dorcas S.
    1997   *Stars of the First People: Native American Star Myths and Constellations.* Pruett: Boulder.

Sueoka, Tomio 末岡外美夫
    1979   *Stars of the Ainu.* 『アイヌの星』 Asahikawa Municipal Library.

2009　　　*Stars and Legends of the Ainu-tari.*『人間達[アイヌタリ]のみた星座と伝承』Asahikawa: Private Publishing.

Watanabe, Hitoshi 渡辺仁
1972　　　*The Ainu Ecosystem: Environment and Group Structure.* Seattle: University of Washington Press.

Yoshida, Iwao 吉田巖
1952　　　Memoirs of Kosankean Furukawa: Ainu ethnography as told by an old Tokachi Ainu. 「古川コサンケアン翁談叢」*Minzokugaku Kenkyu* 16 (3/4): 300–310.

4 Ethnoastronomy in the Ryukyu Islands

Geography and culture of the Ryukyu Islands

The Ryukyu Islands consist of four regions, which from north to south are comprised of the Amami Archipelago, Okinawa, the Miyako Archipelago, and the Yaeyama Archipelago. Miyako and Yaeyama Archipelagos can be grouped as part of the Sakishima Islands group, which are translated as "islands at the far-end" (Figure 4.1).

Since prehistoric times, the Ryukyu Islands have been influenced by cultures from Japan, Taiwan, the Asian continent, and probably from Southeast Asia as well. After the Gusuku (castle) Period (discussed in the next chapter), an independent Ryukyu kingdom formed. The kingdom maintained its independence until the beginning of the seventeenth century when the

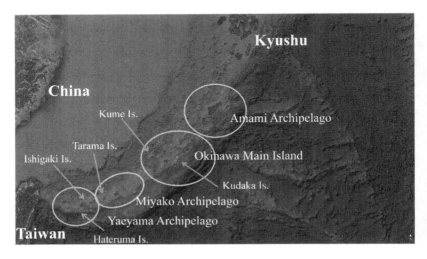

Figure 4.1 Map of Ryukyu Islands.

islands were subordinated to the Japanese Tokugawa government. Before the subordination, the Ryukyu Kingdom prospered through trade with China, Korea, and Southeast Asia (see Chapter 8 for further discussion).

One of the most important aspects of religion in the Ryukyu Islands is that there was little influence of either Buddhism or Shintoism. In contrast, one aspect of Okinawan religion is based on shamanism, in which women are viewed as more sacred than men and women religious specialists have been responsible for many aspects of religious life. In addition, the burial type of the Ryukyu Islands is different from those of Buddhist burials found in Japan. The large burials found in Okinawa are often called "turtle shell" burials, whose origins can be traced to southern China. In addition to these burials, local people originally seem to have used natural caves and the most primitive burial form is a type of cave burial.

In 1868, the newly formed Meiji government succeeded the Tokugawa government after a civil war in Japan. At the end of the nineteenth century, the Meiji government forced the Okinawan people to adopt Shintoism, but local people have continued practicing traditional religion based on shamanism until today. For instance, although Shinto entrances are often situated in front of traditional shrines known as *utaki* 御嶽, today the inside of the *utaki*s remain unchanged. At the very end of *utaki* shrines is the most sacred zone where only shamans are allowed to enter. Here, there are sacred incense burners and a sacred rock (*ibi*), which is considered the chair of the sacred spirit.

Due to the minor influence of Buddhism and Shintoism, traditional beliefs and oral history in the Ryukyu Islands possibly retain some ancient elements of Japanese culture before the influence of Buddhism. Additionally, besides obvious Chinese influence, possible Austronesian influence has also been pointed out from archaeology, linguistics, genetics, and mythology (e.g., Goto 2011; Yoshinari 2018).

Vernacular name of stars

Spring

In spring, the Okinawan people see Centaurus and Crux, which are not visible in other parts of Japan. Centaurus is called *uma no fa bushi*: *uma* (horse) indicates south (see the following star chart), and this name means "stars in the south." α and β of Centaurus are also called *hai ka bushi*, literally meaning "star in the south" (*hai* [south], *ka* [of], *bushi* [star]) (Matsumoto and Nagamine 2019: 13).

Crux is called *hata gashira bushi*, "flag head star" (*hata* [flag], *gashira* [head], *bushi* [star]). The upright position of Crux was recognized as a flag head. On the Kuroshima Island of the Yaeyama Archipelago, Crux is called *hai-ga bushi* (*hai* [south], star), the same as Centaurus in other islands, and it has a particular origin story:

> Long ago there lived a woman with four breasts. Since she was so rare, she was taken to the Royal Palace in Shuri, on Okinawa's main island. She said, "If bright stars are seen horizontally in the southern sky, in May or June, please understand that I have ascended to heaven." Thereafter, she never returned, and the people saw these stars rise. The people understood that the lady was dead and had become a goddess in the sky. When this constellation is seen in an upright position, around seven to eight p.m. from May to June, it is the season to harvest rice in Okinawa.
> (from data file of NPO Okinawa Denshowa Shiryo Center)

The Big Dipper is called *nanachi bushi* (*nanachi* [seven], star), which literally means "seven stars." Concerning this constellation, a swan maiden type of folktale exists:

> Seven maidens descended to earth and bathed. A man stole one of the maiden's clothes and forced her to marry him. In another version, she voluntarily married the man. After several years, the lady found her stolen clothes, put them on, and ascended to the sky with her child. She was the eldest sister, but since she was already polluted on the earth, she designated the second sister as the top of the constellation (Alkaid). She became Mizar, the second star of the Big Dipper, and the small star beside Mizar is considered her child.
> (from data file of NPO Okinawa Denshowa Shiryo Center)

Summer

One of the summer stars is *iyutuyâ bushi* (*iyu* [fish], *tuyâ* [fisherman], star) (Nojiri 1973; Nihon no Hoshi Seiza Hayamiban Project 2019). The hooked shape of Scorpio reminded people of a fishhook. This is similar to the way of thinking of the Polynesians, who saw Scorpio as a fishhook by which demigod Maui fished up islands. In a similar way, fishermen in Setouchi Inland Sea called Scorpio *uoturi-boshi*, or "star for angling fish" (Nojiri 1973; Chapter 1).

The Okinawan people also called Vega *chura aguâ bushi* (*chura* [beautiful], *aguâ* [lady], star), meaning "star for a beautiful lady," and Altair as *mama kuwa bushi*, meaning "star of an adoptive child." I am not sure why this star is called *mama kuwa* ("adoptive child," sometimes also called *mama-ko*], but it likely indicates Altair rises with two small stars at both sides (Nojiri 1973; Nihon no Hoshi Seiza Hayamiban Project 2019).

Sagittarius is called *pai nanachi bushi*, which means "seven stars in the south" (*pai* [south], *nanachi* [seven], star). This idea must have come from China. The name ("seven stars in the south") is a contrast to *hokuto-shichisei* ("seven stars in the north"), indicating the Big Dipper (Nojiri 1973; Nihon no Hoshi Seiza Hayamiban Project 2019).

Fall

The people called the Hyades *uma no chira*, meaning "face of horse" (*uma* [horse], *chira* [face]). (Nojiri 1973; Nihon no Hoshi Seiza Hayamiban Project 2019: 12). It is interesting that westerners saw a bull's face in the same constellation. The Pleiades is called *muri-bushi*, or *muri-ka-bushi*, which means "clustered stars." According to Kitao Koichi, the Pleiades is referred to in Okinawa as *muri-bushi* and elsewhere in the Japanese Archipelago as *subaru* or *sumaru* (Kitao 2018).

Winter

Orion's belt is called *tatsuâki bushi* ("*tatsu* [to stand], *âki* [be bright], star). This probably comes from the fact that Orion's Belt rises vertically from the sea. Capella is called *utora* (or *utona* or *utuna*) *bushi*, and when this constellation is seen, the people predict heavy rain (Nojiri 1973; Nihon no Hoshi Seiza Hayamiban Project 2019: 12).

Polar Star and Milky Way

The Polaris is called *nenufa-bushih* (*ne* [mouse = star], *nu* [of], *fa* [direction], star). In contrast *umanofa-bushi* (Centaurus) (*uma* [horse = south], *no* [of], direction, star) means "southern star" (see Figure 4.6). There is a legend that a widow with three children ascended to heaven with her youngest child. Her oldest son climbed the mountain and saw that the Polaris is an incarnation of the mother rising with a small star (his youngest brother) (Nojiri 1973; Nihon no Hoshi Seiza Hayamiban Project 2019: 12).

Before the introduction of the Chinese calendar and *feng shui* (風水) thinking, most likely in the seventeenth century, Ryukyu Islanders mainly used celestial and natural phenomena to predict seasonal and weather changes in agriculture and fishing. For example, since the Ryukyu Islands lie in the northern hemisphere, the Polaris acted as an important index for knowing directions. There is a folk song, whose lyrics read:

> As the boats sailing during nighttime make the Polaris as a direction mark,
> Parents rely on children as a direction mark.

In Okinawa, there is a belief that a human's life span has been determined by a discussion between the Northern Polar Star or Polaris (*nenufa-bushi*) and the Southern Polar Star when the two stars are playing zest. There is, however, no consensus about what the Southern Polar Star refers to, where it is Centaurus (*umanufa-bushi*), Crux, Canopus, etc.

Chant for the applause of stars

In the *Omoro-soshi*, a collection of chants compiled during the fifteenth to sixteenth century, there is a famous chant applauding stars that translates as:

> Oh, rising of crescent/is a god's golden bow
> Oh, rising Venus/is god's golden arrow
> Oh, rising clustered stars (Pleiades) is god's ornamental hairpin
> Oh, rainbow-colored cloud/is the band loved by god.

This chant clearly shows the Ryukyu Islanders' view of stars as sacred objects. Concerning the expression in the last verse, *nochi gumo* (literally meaning "rainbow-colored cloud"), astronomer Norio Kaifu argued that clouds are not visible during night time, so this portion should be understood as meaning the Milky Way (Kaifu 2018: 184). In the Ryukyu dialect, the Milky Was is usually called *tin ga ra*, meaning "heavenly river" (*tin* [heaven], *ga* [of], *ra* [river]). This interpretation is reasonable since the expression *obi* (band) means something long. If this is so, this chant consistently references stars that Okinawan people find most praiseworthy.

Origin of star sand

In the Yaeyama Islands, there is a well-known white sand beach called *hoshi-zuna*, "star sand." This sand originated from Foraminifera shells and there is an origin story told on Taketomi Island:

> Long ago, a heavenly goddess conceived and looked for a place to deliver her child. She found a beautiful beach on Taketomi Island and delivered her babies. The sea god got angry with this since the goddess defiled the sea. The sea god ordered sea snakes to kill all the babies by biting them. It was believed that the star sand was the remnants of dead babies. The goddess felt very sorry about the babies and

told humans to put star sand in the incense burner of Misaki Utaki Shrine. During an annual ritual, the people burned the incense in remembrance of the babies. The smoke ascends to the sky, taking babies' souls to their mother in heaven.

(from data file of NPO Okinawa Denshowa Shiryo Center)

This legend has been told, concerning Misaki Utaki in Taketomi Island (Figure 4.2).

Observing Pleiades

The Pleiades in the Ryukyu Islands

Among the many constellations seen in the islands, the Pleiades are the most important. The Pleiades is called *murikabushi* or *muribushi*, literally meaning "clustered stars" (*muri* [clustered], star). There are many myths and legends about the Pleiades. In addition to a swan maiden myth that is similar to that of Big Dipper cited above, the Okinawa Denshowa Shiryo Center notes famous folktale concerning the Pleiades:

> Since many years ago, farmers of the Yaeyama Archipelago have had to pay a very heavy land tax to government officials. Seeing that this

Figure 4.2 Misaki Utaki, Taketomi Island, Yaeyama Archipelago.

was not just, the King of the Heavens ordered the Northern Seven Stars to rule the Yaeyama Archipelago. However, since none of the stars obeyed the king, the stars were banished to the northern sky. Thereafter, the king ordered the Southern Seven Stars to rule the islands. However, again, because the stars would not follow the king's orders, they were banished to the southern sky.

The King of the Heavens then became enraged and all of the stars felt frightened. Then, the constellation of little stars, *murikabushi*, went before the King and said that "I will undertake the job." The king was pleased and ordered him to pass through the center of the sky. Therefore, *murikabushi* rises from the East Sea, passes through the center of the sky of the Yaeyama Archipelago, and sets in the West Sea.

After that, by observing the position of these stars in the sky every evening, the farmers were able to plan the schedule for farm work and were able to know the proper times for sowing and harvesting good crops. Farmers always sang the song of *Murikabushi-yunta*, "song of Pleiades," after working on their farms. Farmers said that the reason why their village was rich is because they knew the best times for sowing and harvest wheat by observing the position of stars *murikabushi* (Kaifu 2014: 70–72).

Star-observing stones

The Pleiades was perceived as a zenith star in the Yaeyama Archipelago. In particular, the rise of the Pleiades was observed to define the season for planting crops, such as wheat and foxtail millet.

In the Yaeyama Archipelago, local people erected stones for observing the altitude of the Pleiades. The stone in Kohama Island is called *shichi-sadame-ishi*, meaning "a stone for determining the season" (*shichi* [season], *sadame* [to determine or define], *ishi* [stone]), and those stones on Ishigaki Island and Taketomi Island (Figure 4.3) are called *hoshi-mi-isi*, meaning "a stone for observing stars" (*hoshi* [star], *mi* [to observe], stone). The people of these places would sit in front of the stone and observe the altitude of the Pleiades beyond the top of the stone or through the hole in the stone (Figure 4.4a, b). This occurs around November when the Pleiades appear on the eastern horizon at twilight. When the Pleiades reached a certain altitude at twilight in the eastern sky, farmers started to sow wheat. This practice is similar to customs in Micronesia and in the Gilbert Islands in particular (Goto, Ohnishi, and Ishimura 2019).

Figure 4.3 Shichi-sadame Ishi, Kohama Island, Yaeyama Archipelago.

(a) (b)

Figure 4.4 Hoshi-mi-ishi in Yaeyama Archipelago.
Notes
a Ishigaki Island.
b Taketomi Island.

The Pleiades Shrine

As discussed, religious shrines in the Ryukyu Islands are called *utaki*. Among hundreds of *utaki*, there is one called Muribushi-utaki, or "The Pleiades Shrine" (Figure 4.5). This shrine was constructed for worshiping the Pleiades. There is a legend concerning the origin of this shrine:

> One night, a girl of good behavior saw a light descending from the Pleiades. Every night she saw the same strange phenomenon. The people were so impressed by it that they finally went there to find out what it is. They discovered a circular mark with white sand on the ground. They believed that was the mark where gods descended from heaven. They constructed a shrine for the worship of the Pleiades as a god for fertility.
>   (from data file of NPO Okinawa Denshowa Shiryo Center)

Star lore: indigenous star book and star chart

Even after the introduction of the Chinese calendrical system, the indigenous system seems to have been kept intact on remote islands. For instance, the discovery of *Star Book* (or *The Book on How to Observe Stars*) in the Tarama Island of the Miyako Archipelago is one example.

Figure 4.5 Muribushi-Utaki, Ishigaki Island.

This literature records the ways to define the seasons and predict the weather by observing stars (Tarama Sonshi Henshu Iinkai 1993: 331–340). Similar literature has been found on Kume Island, which lies west of Okinawa Main Island, and Hateruma Island in the southernmost part of the Yaeyama Archipelago. Also, there are many proverbs and pieces of folk knowledge that predict weather patterns based on star observations (e.g., Iwasaki 1974). There is also a "star chart" from Hateruma Island.

Examining the *Star Book* and star chart together, I suggest that the rising and falling of stars were used to index seasons, although there are some ambiguities as to whether the stars were observed at sunset or sunrise. The Tarama Island literature indicates that the people observe the heliacal rise and acoustical rise of particular stars in order to know the season (Tarama Sonshi Henshu Iinkai 1993: 330), as shown in Table 4.1.

In Hateruma literature, such expressions as "when the star is first visible" or "when the star is last visible," indicate that the people observe stars at certain positions. For example, expressions such as "*a-ri yudon*" of "*agari-yudon*" are interpreted as a heliacal rise and "*iri-yudon*" is interpreted as a helical set (Kuroshima 1999). Here, *agari* means "rise" and *iri* means "set," while *yudon* means "stagnation" or "less visible."

In addition, there is also evidence that the rise and set positions of stars were used for telling direction (Table 4.2). In the star chart found on Hateruma Island, it is clearly indicated that stars are used to indicate the direction (Figure 4.6). In the charts, 12 cardinal points are shown and each point is associated with the 12 zodiac animals: north is a mouse, south is a horse, and so on. These 12 animals are also associated with divisions of time in a day: the mouse is midnight, the horse is noon, and so on. These 12 animals also correspond to the 12 years cycle.

This 12-unit system is a modification of the Chinese zodiac system and a similar system was used in Japan as well. From this, we can hypothesize that Ryukyu Islanders used to observe rising and setting points of particular stars as a compass in a similar way to that of the Micronesian star chart.

Sun stone

As will be discussed in the following chapter, the sun was an important symbol of political power in royal ideology. Kume Island, which lies southwest of Okinawa Main Island, was an important location on the trading route between the capital city of Shuri and China. On this island, a high-status man called Donohiya 堂之比屋 is believed to have existed. This man might have occupied a chiefly status and, according to legends, he went to China and learned about the Chinese calendar and astronomy.

Table 4.1 Heliacal rise and acoustic rise of stars, Tarama Island (based on Kuroshima 1999)

Rising

Literature/Star Name	Ko-Yochya bushi (Delphinus)	Oo-Yochya bushi (Pegasus)	Kaboshi bushi (α, β, γ Taurus)	Mutsu bushi (Pleiades)	Utona bushi (Capella)	Mmo bushi (Aldebaran)	Tasisuaki bushi (Orion's Belt)	Futatsu bushi (Gemini)	Oo-Ura bushi (Sirius)
Seizu	7/10–7/end	8/1–8/20	9/1–9/20	9/20–10/10	10/10–10/end	11/1–11/20	11/20–12/10	12/10–1/1	1/1–1/20
Tenkimiyo no koto	7/10–7/15	8/10–8/15	8/27–9/3	10/1–10/10	10/10–10/20	10/20–11/1	11/7–11/10	11/23–12 middle	12/20–1/1
Hoshimiyo (Hateruma I.)	7/10–7/15	8/10–8/15	8/27–9/3	10/1–10/10	10/10–10/20	10/20–11/1	11/7–11/10	11/25–12/10	12/20–1/1
Hoshimiyo (Tarama I.)	7/1–7/15 (Ko-sashi bushi)	8/20–unspecified (Oo-sashi bushi)	9/1–9/4 or 5	10/1–10/5 or 6	10/10– unspecified	10/20– unspecified	11/5 or 6–11/10	11/25 or 26–12/10 (Ubura bushi)	unspecified

Setting

Star Name Literature	Ko-Yochya bushi (Delphinus)	Oo-Yochya bushi (Pegasus)	Kaboshi bushi (α, β, γ Taurus)	Mutsu bushi (Pleiades)	Utona bushi (Capella)	Mmo bushi (Aldebaran)	Tasisuaki bushi (Orion's Belt)	Futatsu bushi (Gemini)	Oo-Ura bushi (Sirius)
Seizu	1/20–2/10	2/10–3/1	3/10–4/1	4/7 or 8–5/1	–	5/1–5/20	5/25–6/20	6/20–7/10	6/25–7/20
Tenkimiyo no koto	1/10–2/1	2/10–3/5 or 6	3/10–4/1	4/7 or 8–5/1	–	5/1–5/20	5/25–6/20	6/20–7/10	6/25–7/20
Hoshimiyo (Hateruma I.)	1/10–2/1	2/10–3/5 or 6	3/10–4/1	4/7 or 8–5/1	–	5/1–5/20	unreadable–6/20	unreadable–20–7/10	missing
Hoshimiyo (Tarama I.)	–	–	–	–	–	–	–	–	–

Table 4.2 Rise and set directions of stars (based on Kuroshima 1999)

Direction													
Star Name	Ko-Yochiya bushi (Delphinus)		Oo-Yochiya bushi (Pegasus)		Nanatsu bushi (Big Dipper)		Kaboshi bushi (α, β, γ Taurus)			Mutsu bushi (Pleiades)	
Literature	Rise	Set	Rise	Set	Rise	Set	Rise	Set		Rise	Set
Seizu	Tiger-Rabitt	Rooster	Tiger	Monkey	Cow	Wild Pig	Tiger			Tiger	Rooster
Tenkimiyo no koto	Tiger-Rabitt	Rooster	Tiger	Monkey	Cow	Wild Pig	Tiger	Rooster		Tiger	Rooster
Hoshimiyo (Hateruma I.)	Tiger-Rabitt	Rooster	Tiger	Monkey			Tiger	Rooster		Tiger	
Hoshimiyo (Tarama I.)	Tiger-Rabitt		Tiger		Cow		Tiger			Tiger	

	Star Name	Utona bushi (Capella)		Mino bushi (Aldebaran)		Tastsuaki bushi (Orion Belt)		Futatsu bushi (Gemini)		Oo-Ura bushi (Sirius)	
Literature	Rise	Set	Rise	Set	Rise	Set	Rise	Set	Rise	Set
Seizu	Cow-Tiger	Wild Pig	Tiger	Rooster	Rabbit	Rooster	Rabbit	Rooster	Rabbit	Rooster
Tenkimiyo no koto	Cow-Tiger	Wild Pig	Tiger	Rooster	Rabbit	Rooster	Rabbit-Cow	Rooster	Rabbit	Rooster
Hoshimiyo (Hateruma I.)	Cow-Tiger		Tiger		Rabbit		Rabbit		Rabbit	
Hoshimiyo (Tarama I.)	Cow-Tiger		Tiger		Rabbit(-Dragon)		Tiger-Rabbit			

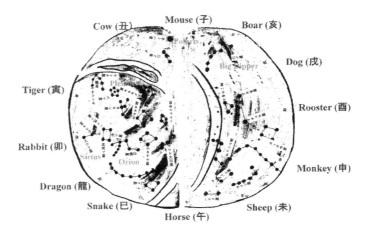

Figure 4.6 Star chart, Hateruma Island.
Source: modified from Kuroshima 1999.

They say that Donohiya specialized in astronomy and navigation, and led the people by predicting weather and seasons. This practice is called *uteda-ugami*, which means to worship or observe (*ugami*) the sun (*teda*) (Nakahara 1990; Goto 2011).

Relatedly, there also exists an *uteda-ishi* stone, which translates as "sun stone." Legend has it that Donohiya used this stone to measure the orbit of the sun. There are grooves on this stone and the direction of grooves seems to point to the rising position of the sun at certain times of the year (Figure 4.7a).

Nakahara mentions the location of this stone (Nakahara 1990). The stone is located at the northernmost peninsula of the island. The reason why the stone is situated far from Donohiya's residence is that the peninsular was an ideal position to observe June and December solstices. From this point, the sun of June solstice rises exactly behind Aguni Island, and the sun of December solstice rises behind Kuba Island (Figure 4.7b). If the stone was situated in a different place on the island, this relation does not work.

I have observed the summer (June) solstice sunrise from this stone on June 22, 2016 (Figure 4.7c and 4.7d), but it seems impossible to observe the winter (December) solstice sunrise from this stone because of heavy vegetation.

Thus, in the Ryukyu Islands, people observed the rise and fall of stars such as the Pleiades and the sun to know the seasons and tell direction (for

Figure 4.7 Sun stone, Kume Island.

Notes
a Sun Stone in Kume Island.
b Direction of solstice sun rinse points seen from sun stone.
c Aguni Island seen from sun stone in Kume Island.
d Summer solstice sunrise behind Aguni Island.

navigation) in their everyday lives. Similar customs probably existed in other parts of Japan before the introduction of the Gregorian calendar and the magnetic compass. More comparative study is needed with tropical islands such as Micronesia and Polynesia.

References

Goto, Akira
    2011   Archaeoastronomy and ethnoastronomy in the Ryukyu Islands: a preliminary report. In: Ruggles, C. (ed.), *Archaeoastronomy and ethnoastronomy: Building Bridges between Cultures*. Cambridge: Cambridge University Press.

Goto, Akira, Ohnishi Hideyuki, and Ishimura, Tomo
   2019   A report on the reassessment of navigation stones on Arorae Kiribati. *People and Culture in Oceania* 35: 109–112.

Iwasaki, Takuji 岩崎卓爾
   1974   *Collected Papers of Takuji Iwasaki in One Volume*. 『岩崎卓爾一巻全集』、Tokyo: Dentoto-Gendaisha.

Kaifu, Norio 海部宣男
   2014   *Stories of Stars in Asia: Mythgs and Legends of Stars and Cosmos in East Asia and the Pacific*. 『アジアの星物語：東アジア・太平洋地域の星と宇宙の神話・伝説』. Tokyo: Manshosha.
   2018   *A Glossary of Seasonal Terms for Astronomy*. 『天文歳時記』 Tokyo: Kadokawa Shoten.

Kitao, Koichi 北尾浩一
   2018   *Encyclopedia of Japanese Star Names*. 『日本の星名事典』 Tokyo: Hara Shobo.

Kuroshima, Tamekazu 黒島為一
   1999   Star chart, weather book, and star book. 「『星圖』『天気見様之事』『星見様（仮題）』」 *Yaeyama Hakubutsukan Kiyo* 16/17: 38–52.

Matsumoto, Tsuyoshi and Nagamine, Miki 松本剛 長嶺美来
   2019   Stars of Ryukyu 「琉球の星」 In: Stars of Japan Project: *Commentary Book of Stars of Japan and Star Chart*. 「日本の星」星座早見盤制作プロジェクト『日本の星座早見盤 解説書』、Stars of Japan Star Chart Project.

Nakahara, Zenshu 仲原善秀
   1990   *History and Folklore of Kumejima Island* (ed. by Hitoshi Uezu). 『久米島の歴史と民俗』（上江洲均編） Tokyo: Daiichi Shobo.

Nihon no Hoshi Seiza Hayamiban Project 日本の星星座版プロジェクト
   2019   Stars of Japan Project: *Commentary Book of Stars of Japan and Star Chart*. 「日本の星」星座早見盤制作プロジェクト『日本の星座早見盤解説書』.

Nojiri, Hoei 野尻抱影
   1973   *A Dictionary of Japanese Star Names*. 『日本星名辞典』 Tokyo: Chuokoronsha.

Tarama Sonshi Henshu Iinkai [Tarama Village History Editorial Board] 多良間村史編集委員会
   1993   *A History of Tarama Village*, Vol. 4 (3): Folklore. 『多良間村史 4巻 (3)：民俗編』 Tarama Village Board of Education.

Yoshinari, Naoki 吉成直樹
   2018   *Kingship and King of the Sun in Ryukyu*. 『琉球王権と太陽の王』 Tokyo: Shichigatsusha.

5 Archaeoastronomy of prehistoric Japan
A historical survey

Introduction

In Japan, the Palaeolithic Period (∼38,000 BCE and earlier) was followed by Jomon Period 縄文時代, which started in 16,000 BCE and lasted more than 12,000 years. The Jomon Period was then followed by the Yayoi Period 弥生時代 (1000 BCE–CE 300), when rice cultivation was established throughout Japan, except in Japan's northernmost island of Hokkaido. After the Yayoi Period, came the Kofun Period 古墳時代, which began around the third century CE and lasted until the seventh century, when the political structure of the Japanese islands shifted toward unification.

In Hokkaido, where rice cultivation was still impossible, the Post-Jomon Culture 続縄文文化 succeeded the Jomon Culture and a foraging economy continued. In this environment, Hokkaido's indigenous hunter–gatherers, the Ainu, emerged throughout Hokkaido (Goto 2018; see Chapter 7).

Pioneer studies by British scholars

William Gowland was a British mining engineer who was invited to Japan to teach mining technology in the late nineteenth century. He was familiar with surveying technology and as a hobby he would visit archaeological sites during his holidays. He introduced scientific surveying techniques to the ancient burial mounds or *kofun* (tumuli) and he is now referred to as the "father of Japanese archaeology or Kofun studies" (Asahi Shimbun and British Museum 2003).

In two scientific papers, Gowland noted that the burial chamber of *kofun* tends to be opened to the south, regardless of topography. He argued that this trend was due to sun worship by the ancient people of Japan. He wrote:

> The reasons which have been advanced for the southern aspect of tombs are well known to archaeologists and need not be adduced here. I may, however, say briefly that in Japan its origin has probably some basis on the ancient sun-worship, of which here are many survivals in the country. The influence of the sun was believed to be beneficent to the spirits, hence these chambers of the dead were directed towards its meridional position.
>
> (Gowland 1897: 451)

Concerning the southern orientation of burial chambers, he further argued in another paper:

> Like the rude stone monuments of other races, all dolmens, of whatever class, with few exceptions, are built in a definite direction, and whether they occur singly or in groups, have an approximately southern aspect. In the province of Iyo only there is an absence of this uniformity in orientation, and they there face almost every point of the compass.
>
> (Gowland 1899: 132–133)

> There is, too, no absolutely conclusive evidence of sun worship, although some particular virtue appears to have been attached to the south point of the compass, as there are so many examples of dolmens in which, in order to obtain a southern aspect on the slopes of some hills, the difficulties of construction must have been enormous, whilst with another bearing there would have been none. Neither is there any object to show that the phallic worship of later times prevailed.
>
> (Gowland 1899: 169–170)

After returning to England, Gowland applied Japanese customs to the interpretation of Stonehenge (Gowland 1902: 8). He mentioned the worship of summer solstice sunrise at Meoto Iwa 夫婦岩 (Husband-Wife Rock) in Futamiga-ura 二見浦 of Ise, and he used Japanese techniques to transport heavy rocks as an ethnographic analogy for transporting heavy rocks to Stonehenge. Today, his method is understood as ethnoarchaeology.

Interestingly, Norman Locker, a pioneer of modern archaeoastronomy, was impressed with Gowland's discussion of Meoto Iwa and believed that this Japanese custom was a remnant of sun worship that had already disappeared in Egypt and Britain. In that drawing, Lockyer noticed a *torii* 鳥居, an entrance gate of a Shinto shrine, and referred to the *torii* as "trilithon" similar to stone structures used in Stonehenge (Gowland 1902: 88; cited by Lockyer 1906: 16–17). Citing Gowland, Locker wrote:

Archaeoastronomy of prehistoric Japan 65

> There on the seashore at *Fûtami-ga-ura* (as will be seen in the copy of a print which I obtained at that ancient place), the orientation of the shrine of adoration is given by two gigantic rocks which rise from the sea as natural pillars. The sun, as it rises over the mountain of the distant shore, is observed between them and the customary prayers and offerings made in that direction.
>
> (Lockyer 1906: 16)

Locker further argued about the symbolic meaning of these rocks:

> It is, too, specially worthy of note that the point from which the sun is revered is marked by a structure of the form of a trilithon but made of wood and placed immediately behind the altar. This representative of the trilithon is of very remote date in Japan and has been in use from the earliest times in connection with the observance of the ancient Shintô cult in which the Sun-Goddess is the chief deity. One of its important uses, which still survives, was to indicate the direction of the position of some sacred place or object of veneration, in order that worshippers might make their prayers and oblations towards the proper quarter.
>
> (Lockyer 1906: 16–17)

This practice continues today (Figure 5.1).

Figure 5.1 June Solstice sunrise from Futamiga-ura, Ise (June 22, 2017).

In addition to Gowland, Neil Munro, a British medical doctor, was another pioneer of archaeoastronomy in Japan. During his career, Munro studied artifacts and skeletal remains in the Tokyo area. During the 1930s, he married a Japanese woman and became a naturalized Japanese citizen. He then moved to Hokkaido, the homeland of the Ainu, and continued to study Ainu culture (Munro 1961).

In his book titled *Prehistoric Japan*, Munro analyzed the orientation of the stone circle of Oshoro in Otaru, a city in Hokkaido, and argued that the structure carried an astronomical significance. He suggested that the stone circle was a specialized burial in which human sacrifice was practiced (Munro 1908: 637). He further wrote: "It is not improbable that this cyclolith was oriented for a particular date of sunrise but this has not yet been definitely ascertained" (Munro 1908: 638).

In his book, Munro, citing Gowland's study of *kofun*, wrote:

> It is yet too early to hazard a guess as to whether the orientation was carefully arranged for a particular date of sunrise, or whether the departures that are noticed are accidental, or due to some other circumstances. Though in the case of caves, the choice of position was more restricted, there is here also a very decided orientation towards the south in the vast majority of cases.
>
> (Munro 1908: 383–384)

Jomon burial orientation

One of the earliest Japanese attempts of archaeoastronomy focused on the burial orientations found in Jomon shell mounds. Japanese archaeologists have analyzed burial orientation together with other factors, such as the pose of the buried body (e.g., extended vs. flexed burial), laying position (face up, face sideways, etc.), the difference of buried zones, types of offerings, and the age and sex of the buried persons, among others.

Hasebe Kotondo, a leading physical anthropologist of that time, discovered an eastern orientation of the heads of buried persons in Jomon shell mounds. He argued that the reason why the head was oriented to the east does not mean that the Jomon people considered the east important, but rather it was a custom in which the dead people would look to the western sky when they were resurrected. He argued that a similar custom is found in the Pre-Modern Ainu and groups in Siberia, and it was related to the belief that sunlight causes the dead to resurrect (Hasebe 1920).

Others arrived at similar conclusions. Ogushi Kikujiro suggested that the burials found in Tzugumo Shell Mound 津雲貝塚 and the Kou Site 国府 were largely oriented to the east, regardless of the topography. He argued that the orientation was related to the rise of the sun and moon (Ogushi 1920). However, Koganei Ryosei, admitting that the eastern orientation of burials is dominant, noted there is regional variation and the topography (slope) was equally important (Koganei 1923). Kiyono Kenji recognizing the relationship between burial orientation and topography, and argued that the eastern orientation of burials was more related to sun worship than to topography (Kiyono 1946: 129).

Okamoto Isam, citing an ethnography by Henry Morgan, argued that the difference of burial orientation was related to social organization, such as clan differences (Okamoto 1956: 328). Okamoto did not refer to pages on Morgan's book, but the following is most likely the pages on Morgan's book that Okamoto cited:

> in a particular cemetery, members of all the gentes established in a village would be buried; but they might keep those of the same gens locally together ... individuals of the same gens are buried in a row by themselves ... One row is composed of the graves of the deceased members of the Beaver gens, two rows of the members of the Bear gens, one row of the Gray Wolf ...
>
> (Morgan 1877: 84)

During the 1960s, Ohtsuka Kazuyoshi overviewed burial orientations found in northern Japan. He noted that northwestern burial orientation was distributed from Hokkaido to northern Tohoku in the Late Jomon Period and that this distribution largely overlaps with those of stone circles. From the Late Jomon Period to the Post-Jomon Period, burial orientations in Hokkaido were divided into two patterns: northwestern and southeastern. Ohtsuka argued that the temporal shift of burial orientation was related to the strength of astronomical ideology (Ohtsuka 1967).

During the 1960s to 1970s, one of the leading figures of archaeoastronomy was Fujimoto Hideo. He was a high school teacher in Shizunai Town 静内町 in Hokkaido. While advising a local history club at his high school, he excavated important burial sites of the Jomon Period and other periods (see Chapter 7).

A special mention should be made of Gotenyama Burial 御殿山 site belonging to the Final Jomon Period, where burials were mostly oriented to the west. The orientations of Gotenyama Burial tend to be within the solstice range (Figure 5.2a) and Fujimoto argued that this custom was related to sun worship among the Jomon people (Fujimoto 1964, 1971).

Fujimoto's analysis seems to have been based on magnetic north. A recent computer simulation by Hojo Yoshitaka considering the effect of precession has indicated that true north was about 9 degrees east of "north"

68 Archaeoastronomy of prehistoric Japan

(a)

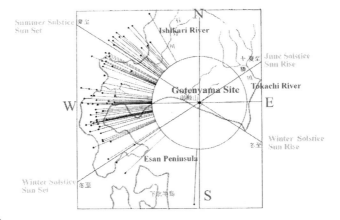

(b)

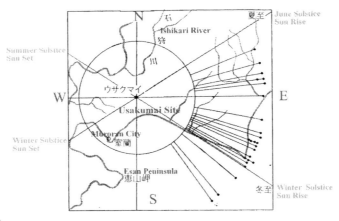

Figure 5.2 Burial orientation in Hokkaido Sites.

Source: Fujimoto 1971: 157 & 182.

Notes
a Gotenyam Site (40°19' N).
b Usakumai Site (42°50' N).
*SSR Summer Solstice Sunrise Direction, WSR: Winter Solstice Sunrise Direction.
 SSS Summer Solstice Sunset Direction, WSS: Winter Solstice Sunset Direction.

in Fujimoto's drawing. As a result, most of the burial orientation ranges within sunset points between summer and winter solstices (Hojo, personal communication).

Similar western orientation was also found in other sites, such as Sakkari 札苅, Kashiwagi 柏木, and others (Fujimoto 1987). In the Takasago Shell Mound 高砂貝塚, most orientations are western-oriented, but one faces the east. The eastern-oriented burial was for a woman with bones around her femur and the bones were from a fetus, eight to nine months old. The Ainu had a custom in which they would cut the belly of the woman who died before delivery. They then took out the baby in order to remove the pain of the mother. Thereafter, the mother was believed to proceed to the afterworld safely. Fujimoto argued that this "abnormal" burial was for somebody who died an unnatural death (Fujimoto 1964: 183; 1971: 203).

Fujimoto argued that the western orientation of Jomon burials is also found in the Kashiko Dodokoro Shall Mound 柏子所貝塚 of Akita Prefecture in northern Tohoku and also in the Esan Shell Mound 恵山貝塚 of the Post-Jomon Period (Fujimoto 1964: 186). In the later Post-Jomon Period (e.g., Kohoku 後北), there appeared burials orienting to the east (Fujimoto 1971). Fujimoto believed that this eastern orientation was characteristic of the Satsumon Culture, a typical example came from Usakumai Site (Figure 5.2b). Fujimoto further argued that this custom had been inherited by the Pre-Modern Ainu (Fujimoto 1971: 182; see also Chapter 8).

Some researchers have critically examined the arguments offered by Ohtsuka and Fujimoto, and they came to believe that burial orientation was just one factor to be integrated with others in the analysis, such as the of patterns of *basshi* 抜歯 (tooth extraction) found on buried skulls (e.g., Watanabe 1969; Harunari 1983).

Hayashi Kensaku reanalyzed the burial orientations at Jomon sites, including Gogenyama and Kashiko Dokoro, and argued that the orientation of burials was more dispersed than Fujimoto had previously shown. Hayashi argued that orientations tend to be clustered into two or more groups and that these groups correspond to dualism philosophy 双分制原理 and/or some kind of social units, such as clans (Hayashi 1977a, 1977b).

In the reanalysis of burial orientations from the Sanganji Shellmond 三貫地貝塚 (Mori 1988) of Fukushima Prefecture, folklorist Sasaki Chosei argued that the regularity of burial orientation is related to the direction of a sacred mountain, Karosan Mountain 鹿狼山, which lies north-northwest of the site (Sasaki 1988; cf. Hayashi 1977a) (Figure 5.3).

Similar tendencies (burials oriented toward sacred mountains) are also observed in the Tenjin Bara Site 天神原 and the Nakanoya Matsubara Site 中野谷松原 in Gunma Prefecture (Daikubara and Sekine 2001). The strong tendency of solstice-orientation of burial is also pointed out in

70 *Archaeoastronomy of prehistoric Japan*

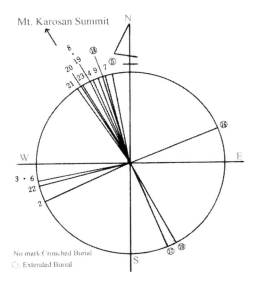

Figure 5.3 Burial orientation at Sanganji Site.

Source: modified from Mori 1988, Figure 245a.

Genjoudaira Site 源常平 of Aomori Prefecture, northern Japan (Nishida 1996: 107) (Figure 5.4).

To summarize of the study of Jomon burial orientations from the 1940s to 1990s, there have been three major interpretations of burial orientations (Yamada 2003): (1) astronomical interpretations (sun worship), (2) social interpretations (different clusters of burial orientation corresponding to social units) and dualism philosophy, and (3) cosmological interpretations: e.g., the direction of sacred mountain). In particular, after World War II and until the 1970s, when Japanese archaeology had become a professional discipline, astronomical interpretations were avoided (cf. Hutton 2013), although astronomical and cosmological interests have never fully diminished.

Jomon stone circles

Besides burial orientations, one of the earliest attempts by Japanese researchers was on the astronomical analysis of the Oyu Stone Circles 大湯環状列石 in Akita (Togashi 1995: 31). These monuments have been called the sundials of the Jomon Era. This site consists of two stone circles, Nonakado 野中堂 Circle and Manza 万座 Circle, with other stone structures including the so-called sundial and others (Figure 5.5a and 5.5b).

Archaeoastronomy of prehistoric Japan 71

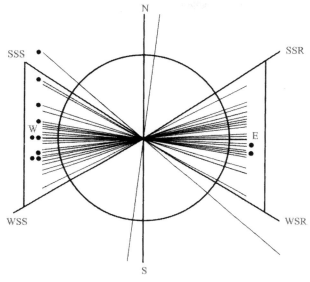

• Estimated Head Orientation

Figure 5.4 Burial orientation at Genjodaira Site.
Source: modified from Nishida 1996, figure on p. 107.

Amateur archaeologist Kawaguchi Shigekazu asked an astronomer to estimate the orientation of the sunset point about 5,000 years ago, during the Late Jomon Era. He then concluded that the western extension lied between the center of the two stone circles and was directed toward the sunset point at June solstice (Kawaguchi 1956) (Figure 5.5c).

Although archaeologists have not yet determined whether two stone circles were contemporaneous, it is highly probable that the lines that connected the centers of the two stone circles and stone structures in the northwest were directed toward the sunset point at June solstice at that time (Togashi 1995). Excavations conducted around these circles have revealed burials and housing sites around them, and the debate is still ongoing concerning the function of these circles (whether they were ritual places or burials) (Akimoto 2005).

Physicist Sago Tsutomu conducted a geometrical analysis of the two stone circles belonging to the Oshoro Stone Circles, which Munro studied at the beginning of the twentieth century (Munro 1908) (Figure 5.6a and 5.6b). They applied Alexander Thom's analytical method and deduced several significant lines from the stone circle (Figure 5.6c). They then

72 *Archaeoastronomy of prehistoric Japan*

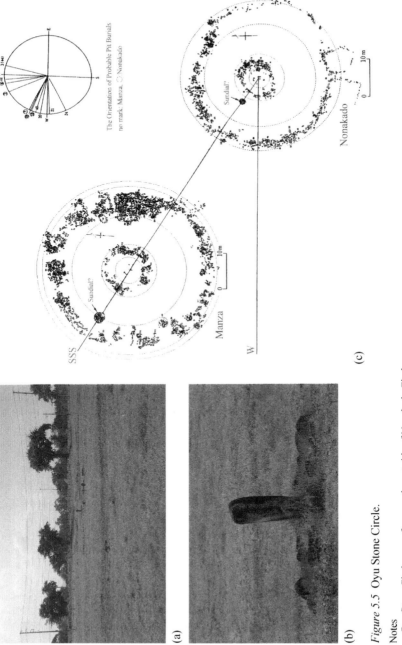

Figure 5.5 Oyu Stone Circle.

Notes
a Oyu Stone Circles seen from south-east side of Nonakado Circle.
b So called sundial.
c: Plan of Oyu Stone Circles (modified from Togashi 1995: Fig. 3).

Archaeoastronomy of prehistoric Japan 73

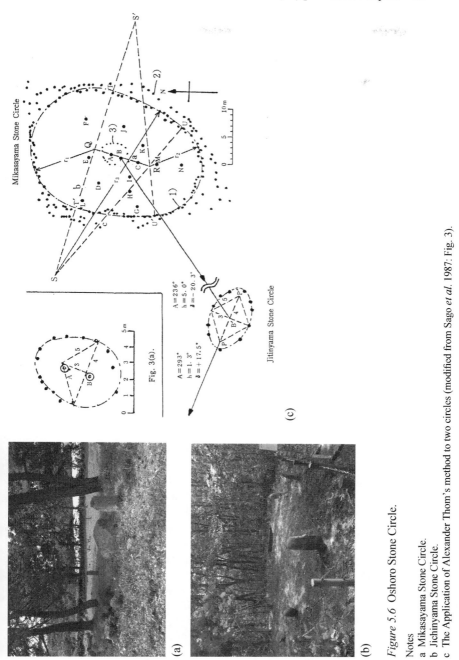

Figure 5.6 Oshoro Stone Circle.
Notes
a Mikasayama Stone Circle.
b Jichinyama Stone Circle.
c The Application of Alexander Thom's method to two circles (modified from Sago et al. 1987: Fig. 3).

related these lines to several astronomical phenomena: (1) sunrise and sunset at solstices and equinoxes, (2) maximum standstill of the Moon and setting or rising points of Capella, Spica, Betelgeus, Rigel and others. They further argued that some lines were related to the constellations that are not visible today but were visible at that time due to presession: they were the Southern Cross and the Centaurus (Sago, Yamada and Borst 1986).

In the 1990s, Kobayashi Tatsuo and his colleagues analyzed the alignments of Jomon settlements, including stone circles, with the aid of computer simulation software (Kobayashi 2005). These studies were titled "Jomon Landscape Studies" and revealed that Jomon people were possibly aware of astronomical phenomena when they designed the settlement.

In addition, there were many stone circles and monuments (e.g., sacred rocks called *iwakura* 磐座) found throughout the Japanese Archipelago, which some professional and amateur researchers argue to have had an astronomical significance (Kobayashi and Tokuda 2016). More extensive analysis is required to reach a conclusive result.

Yayoi settlement studies

Concerning the Yayoi Period, Harada Dairoku conducted pioneer studies at the Hirabaru Site 平原遺跡 in Fukuoka, northern Kyushu (Harada 1966). This site belongs to the final phase of the Yayoi Period, where abundant bronze mirrors have been found. In this site, one burial with a wooden coffin was excavated. Around the burial mound, a pair of post holes were found. Harada considered that this pair of holes were for a *torii* 鳥居 and he identified three pairs of similar post holes.

From a *torii* that lay on the main axis of the burial mound, we can see Hinata Pass 日向峠. It is on October 20 when the sun is seen to rise on this pass (Figure 5.7a). Harada argued that the sunbeam on this day shines on the crotch of the dead who was probably a sun priestess, like Queen Himiko 卑弥呼, who was believed to have been conceived by sunlight (Figure 5.7b). From another *torii*, we can see the summit of Mt. Koso 高祖山 and Harada argued that this site was used for observing the movements of sunrise during the agricultural calendar (Figure 5.7c).

Hojo Yoshitaka recently reanalyzed the alignment of this site and found that the day when the sun rose from the summit of Humuka Pass was not October 20 but October 22 (Figure 5.7d). Moreover, he argued that the same phenomenon happens on February 20 also and that these two days were both important days for annual ceremonies concerning rice cultivation. These ceremonies are still held at Ise Shrine, which is one of the most important Shinto shrines in Japan (Hojo 2017: 25–26, 211–232).

Archaeoastronomy of prehistoric Japan 75

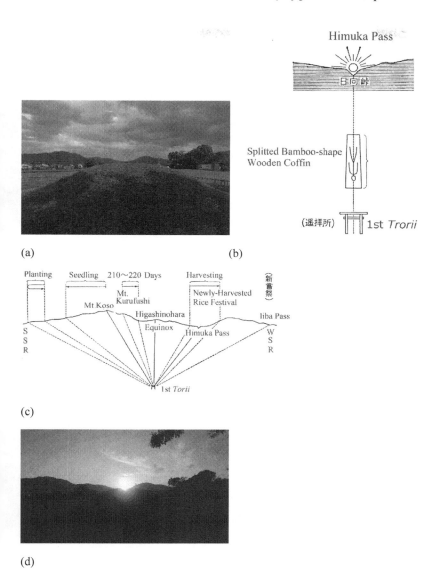

Figure 5.7 Hirabaru site, Fukuoka.

Notes
a Hinata Pass seen from Main Burial Mound.
b Estimated Mechanism of the sun and burial (modified from Harada 1966: p. 145).
c Rice Farming Calendar in Hirabaru Site (modified from Harada 1966: p. 135).
d Sun rise behind Hinata Pass, October 22, 2019, 6:42 a.m.: courtesy of Tsujita Junichiro.

The Yoshinogari Site 吉野ヶ里 in Saga Prefecture, also in Kyushu, is one of the most famous settlements of the Yayoi Period and a whole village has been excavated at this site (Figure 5.8a). Here, archaeologists discovered dwelling houses, storage houses, communal structures, ritual grounds, burial mounds, and pit burials, as well as various other important articles (Figure 5.8b). The main axis that connects the burial mounds and ritual ground in the northern section and the mound structure in the south seems to have been directed toward the summit of a volcano, Mt. Unzen Fugen 雲仙普賢岳. Shichida Tadaaki, who led the excavation, argued that the basic alignment of the settlement was originally directed toward Mt. Unzen Fugen, but he found that in later periods another alignment had been added to an enclosed settlement full of religious structures, whose main axis was probably directed to the summer solstice sunrise or winter solstice sunset (Shichida 2012) (Figure 5.8c).

Astronomical considerations of solstice and equinox sunrise points, and the directions of sacred mountains, have also been proposed to exist in Karako Kagi 唐古鍵遺跡 settlements in the Nara Basin of central Japan, where the first unitary dynasty of Japan emerged. This site had been occupied for a long time, since the early Yayoi Period until the early Kofun Period. It has already been pointed out that when viewed from the site, December solstice sun rose behind a sacred mountain of Mt. Miwa 三輪山. By conducting computer simulations on the timing of when the middle point of the solar disc first appeared behind mountain ridge, Hojo argued that the equinox sun rose behind Mt. Ryuo Zan 竜王山 and June solstice sun rose from Mt. Takahashi 高橋山. These phenomena would be important to signal seasonal calendar rice farming (Hojo 2017: 183–193).

Kofun structure and orientation

Kofun studies, which Gowland pioneered and had been further developed by Japanese archaeologists, have found several types of burial mounds: rectangular, circular, keyhole shape (square at the front and rounded in the rear), squares both at the front and in the rear type, and several others. The following discussion examines the keyhole-shaped mounds, whose construction started at the beginning of the Kofun Period (late third century) and contains many giant mounds that were likely royal tombs.

Here, I would like to mention that the main axis of the burial mounds and the orientation of burial chambers do not necessarily correspond with each other. In some cases, burial chambers are laid at right angles to the main axis of burial mounds and there is a temporal as well as regional variation in their relationship (e.g., Goto 1936; Kobayashi 1961; Shiraishi 1989; Hojo 2017).

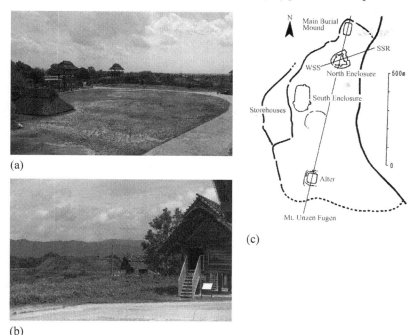

Figure 5.8 Yoshinogari site, Saga.

Notes
a An Overview of Yoshinogari Site.
b Main Burial Mound seen from North Enclosure.
c Plan of the Site (modified from Shichida 2012: Figure 1).

Before World War II, Goto Shuichi was one of the pioneer Japanese archaeologists of Kofun studies. He noticed the temporal shift of the orientation of burial mounds (Goto 1935, 1936). Kobayashi Yukio, critically examining Goto's arguments, pointed out that burial chamber orientation was more diverse, and that the presence/absence of Triangle Rim Beast Mirrors 三角縁神獣鏡 is more important than orientation when considering the social status of the buried, since this type of mirror was the most prestigious item at that age (Kobayashi 1961).

One of the leading figures of Kofun studies from the 1950 to the 1970s was Saito Tadashi. He analyzed some 400 examples from various topographies and suggested that the eastern orientation is similar to the custom of Shilla 新羅 (57 BCE–CE 935) in the eastern part of the Korean Peninsula and the northern orientation to Lelang Commandery 楽浪郡 (108 BCE–CE 313) in the northern part of the Korean Peninsula (Saito 1953).

Saito further argued that the eastern orientation was related to sun worship and that the northern orientation due to the influence of Chinese Confucianism philosophy (Saito 1961).

To summarize, early Japanese researchers following Gowland continued to point out the regularity of the burial orientation of burial mounds, namely eastern and northern orientations, which varied by area. Although most of them recognized the particular orientation of burial mounds and burial chambers, researchers have proposed several different interpretations: topographical, symbolic, political, as well as astronomical.

Topographic interpretations refer to the location of the mounds (such as at the mountain slope) since some early keyhole-shaped mounds were built along mountain ridges by shaving the summit. Thus, the orientation of these mounds tends to accord with the direction of the slope. Political interpretations argue that the difference in burial orientation reflected the social status of buried persons (Hojo 2017: 31). Symbolic interpretations propose that the burial orientations were related to landscape features and, in particular, the direction of the sacred mountain. Symbolic interpretations have often been combined with astronomical ones.

Concerning the coffin chamber orientation in the Kinki area of central Japan, where the first Japanese dynasty appeared, many researchers recognized the dominance of the *kita-makura* 北枕, which is literally translated as "northern pillow." The "northern pillow" suggests that the deceased was buried with his/her head orienting to the north. This is the same as what Gowland called "southern aspect," since the burial chamber is usually opened toward the south. Until today, Japanese customs believe that it is not good to sleep with your head to the north since the "northern pillow" position is a custom reserved only for the dead.

Tsude Hiroshi, citing classic Chinese philosophy that states that "the living people face the south, and the dead people face the north 正者南面、死者北面," argued that this northern pillow custom came from China (Tsude 1979, 1989).

In his recent book, *The Orientation of Kofun and the Sun*, Hojo Yoshitaka reanalyzed astronomical interpretations of *kofun* burial orientations (Hojo 2017). Using astronomical simulations and calculations, Hojo has convincingly shown that the burials characterized as "northern pillow" are mostly laid within a range of the circular movement of the Big Dipper. Since there was not a conspicuous "polar star" during the third to seventh centuries, Hojo has proposed a hypothesis that ancient people observed the circulation of the Big Dipper or observed crossing the meridian of Dubhe or α Big Dipper (*tiān shū* 天枢 in Chinese) and possibly Alkaid or η Big Dipper (*yáo guāng* 摇光) (Figure 5.9a). Figure 5.9b indicates the image of Big Dipper and Ishizuyama Kofun that is the third largest burial mound in Japan.

Archaeoastronomy of prehistoric Japan 79

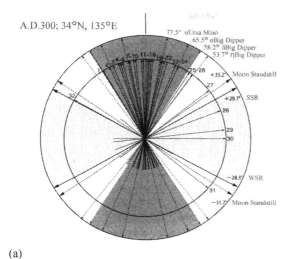

(a)

(b)

Figure 5.9 Orientation of Kofun burial.

Notes
a Orientation of burial chamber of the Early Kofun Period, Kinki Region (modified from Hojo 2017: Figure 3.11).
b The Image of Big Dipper and Ishizuyama Kofun (so called Emperor Richu's Burial) (modified from Hojo 2017: Figure 5.17).

Since the orientation of mounds and/or burial chambers do not show northern orientation in other regions (Shikoku, Kyushu, etc.), we need a more integrated framework and astronomical interpretations should be balanced with topographic, socio-political, and cosmological interpretations.

Kofun painted with star charts

Researchers have found quite a few *kofun* whose burial chamber walls were decorated with colorful paintings, which are referred to as decorated Kofun, *Soshoku Kofun* 装飾古墳. Some of them depict interesting examples of the "the ship of the dead," which was probably believed to transport dead souls to the afterworld. In these depictions, often the symbol of the sun is painted together with birds.

There are two famous *Soshoku Kofun* in which astronomical charts were drawn: Takamatsu Zuka Kofun 高松塚古墳 and Kitora Kofun キトラ古墳 (see Figure 2.3a for their locations). Both of them were constructed in the final phase of the Kofun Period, from the latter part of the seventh or early part of the eighth century. These mounds were aligned with celestial north.

In Takamatsu Zuka, which was discovered in the 1970s, four animals were painted on the walls corresponding to the four cardinal directions: in the north is a *genbu* (black tortoise), east is a *seiryu* (blue dragon), south is a *suzaku* (red bird of summer/phoenix), and west is a *byakko* (white tiger). Also, the chart indicates stars of 28 *Sei Shuku* 星宿 (lunar stations), and evidence clearly shows the influence of Chinese and Korean cosmological thoughts (Figure 5.10a).

In 1998, another *Soshoku Kofun*, Kitora Kofun, was examined. The decoration of Kitora Kofun was similar to that of Takamatsu Zuka Kofun in that four sacred animals were painted on the four walls of the chamber. A white tiger is facing north in Kitora Kofun, but in Takamatsu Zuka Kofun the white tiger was facing south. There are also 28 *Sei Shuku* painted at this site, but unlike Takamatsu Zuka Kofun, the inner cycle within which circumpolar stars were painted, and the celestial equator and ecliptic, were also shown clearly (Figure 5.10b).

Thus, the decoration of both *kofun* was similar, but the paintings of *Sei Shuku* on Kitora Kofun appear to be based on Chinese and Korean charts of a much earlier period than those of Takamatsu Zuka Kofun. In addition, the point of the crossing of the ecliptic with the celestial equator appears to be near a point in Aries closer to Taurus and corresponding with the position several centuries earlier than the Asuka Period when the tombs were constructed. The vernal equinox must have been close to Pisces by the end of the seventh century.

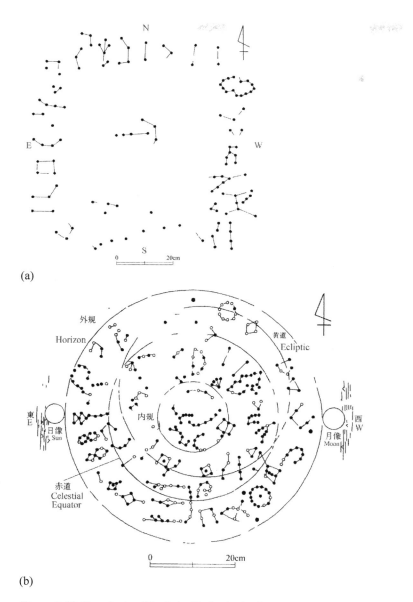

Figure 5.10 Star charts of Soshoku Kofun in Asuka.

Notes
a Star Chart in Takamatzu Zuka Kofun (modified from Izumi 2018: Fig. 9).
b Star Chart in Kitora Kofun (modified from Izumi 2018: Fig. 5).

In contrast with the stylistic star painting at Takamatsu Zuka Kofun, the painting of stars and constellations at Kitora Kofun was much more exact. The examination of stars painted must have shown the visible stars above the horizon and therefore we can estimate the latitude of the observer/painter of this star chart, as well as the age when it was painted.

Astronomer Miyajima Kazuhiko, who analyzed the star chart of Kitora Kofun, argued that this chart reflected the sky abound 65 BCE in the northern Korean Peninsular during the Koguryo Kingdom 高麗 (Miyajima 1999). Recently, Miyajima reanalyzed the offset in declination of the 28 *Sei Shuku* from the heavenly Arctic 去極度 and estimated that the Kitora Kofun star chart reflected the starry sky in the southern zone, such that of as Seoul (Miyajima 2018).

Another astronomer, Nakamura Tsukou, conducted a statistical analysis of the offset in declination of the 28 *Sei Shuku* stars from the heavenly Arctic and offset it in right ascension between the 28 *Sei Shuku*. He concluded that the starry sky painted in Kitora Kofun must have reflected the night sky around 80±40 years BCE (Nakamura 2018: 79). Detailed comparisons of star charts in these two *Soshoku Kofun* with Chinese star charts still continues (Izumi 2018).

Stone monument and star observatory in the Asuka Period: an unsolved issue

As mentioned in Chapter 3, the *Nihonshoki* states that "a platform was for the first time erected from which to divine by means of the stars" (Aston 1972: 326). That was the era of Emperor Tenmu in CE 675. In relation to this description, many discussions have been made of a monument called Masuda Iwafune 益田岩船, since the Edo Period (1681). *Iwafune* literally means "rock-ship" and this rock has two square holes on it. The rock lies on a hill and one possible function of the rock was the observation of stars (Figure 5.11a).

There are many other opinions, however, and one of them claims that the two holes were used to erect wood pillars or stone epitaphs for erecting this rock as some kind of monument. Or it could be the foundation of Amatsu Miya 天宮, Palace of Heaven, that was built by two *tsuki* trees (Palace of *Futa-tuki* 両槻宮) on top of the Tou Peak 多武峯 (Aston 1972, Vol II: 250; Saito 1982: 61).

The main axis of this rock is about 283 degrees and astronomer Kuniji Saito analyzed this rock when the sun sets in this direction. His analysis included not only the direction of the main axis but also western topography and refraction of the air that influences the visibility of the sun.

Archaeoastronomy of prehistoric Japan 83

(a)

(b)

Figure 5.11 Stone monuments in Asuka.

Notes
a Masuda Iwafune.
b Sakafune Ishi.

He concluded that days when the sun set in that direction were 27 days after vernal equinox and 27 days before autumn equinox. He argued that the former date would be important since it corresponds to the date of Vernal Doyo 春の土用, which is one of the 12 minor seasonal points called *zassetsu* 雑節 that divide the seasons of the year. That time was when the solar ecliptic is 27 degrees and Vernal Doyo was important to signal the beginning of rice planting (Saito 1982: 60–61).

Saito also analyzed another enigmatic rock, called Sakafune Ishi 酒船石 (alcohol ship rock) in the same area. The grooves cut on the rock are considered to be related to circulating water, oil, vermilion, or sake (Japanese wine) and the main axis is 283 degrees, exactly corresponding to that of Masuda *iwafune* (Saito 1982: 64) (Figure 5.11b).

Issues in later periods: orientation of Buddhist temples

Archaeoastronomical issues in Japan are not limited to prehistoric periods. Although there are many examples in later periods to be discussed, I will mention just one issue to be explored in the future: the orientation of Buddhist temples.

Buddhist temples have been built since the Asuka Period (CE 592–710) and Ishida Mosaku analyzed the alignment of some 50 temples built in this period. He found that the temples were built along a north-south axis, with the main building facing south but that the basic axes were shifted from four to seven degrees west of south. Since true north is 3 degrees 12" degrees east of magnetic north in Nara, where these temples are located, Ishida argued that temples were built on the basis of true north, observing Polaris (Ishida 1944: 43–44).

Ishida did not mention either precession or a temporal shift of magnetic north. In contrast to Ishida's pioneer analysis, some later researchers argued that the variation in the offset from true north resulted from the change of magnetic north that was used to index north (Hirooka 1976).

Watanabe Naotsune analyzed whether the offset of temple alignment from the Asuka Period to the Medieval Period (seventeenth century) accords with the shift of magnetic north. He concluded that there is not a significant correlation between the axis of the temple alignment and the magnetic north at the age of construction (Watanabe 1959).

However, reanalysis of the correlation, which also considered topographic factors, has indicated that temples tend to have been designed using some kind of device to measure magnetic north. In contrast, it seems that the urban designs of capitals, Fujiwara-kyo 藤原京 (694–710), Heijo-kyo 平城京 (710–784), and Heian-kyo 平安京 (794–1868) were decided by using true north (Hirooka 1976: 56).

Therefore, we need to further explore how these historic Japanese intentionally used true north and magnetic north differently in each situation. Another question concerns what kind of device they used for measuring each.

References

Akimoto, Nobuo 秋元信夫
    2005   *Prayer in Stone of the Jomon People: Oyu Stone Circles.* 『石にこめた縄文人の祈り』 Tokyo: Shisensha.

Asahi Shimbun and British Museum
    2003   *William Gowland: the Father of Japanese Archaeology.* Tokyo: Asashi Simbun and British Museum Press.

Aston W.G.
    1972   *Nihongi: Chronicle of Japan from the Earliest Times to A.D. 697.* Tokyo: Tuttle.

Fujimoto, Hideo 藤本英夫
    1964   *The Burial of the Ainu.* 『アイヌの墓』 Tokyo: Nikkei-Shinbun.
    1971   *The Burial of the North.* 『北の墓』 Tokyo: Gakusei-sha.
    1987   Burial custom and cosmology of the Jomon Period. 「縄文時代の葬制と宇宙観」 In: *An Outline of World Archaeology: Supplement of Japanese Archaeology* 『世界考古学 大系: 日本補遺編』, pp. 53–62. Tokyo: Tenzansha.

Goto, Akira 後藤 明
    2018   House and burial orientations of the Hokkaido Ainu, indigenous hunter-gatherers of northern Japan. *Meditarranean Archaeology and Archaeometry* 18(2): 173–180.

Goto, Shuichi 後藤守一
    1935   On Key-hole tululi. 「前方古墳雑考」 *Rekishi Koron* 4(7): 24–44.
    1936   *An Introduction to Burials*. 『墳墓概説』 Tokyo: Yuzankaku.

Gowland, William
    1897   The dolmens and burial mounds in Japan. *Archaeologia* IV: 439–524.
    1899   The dolmens of Japan and their builders. *Transactions and Proceedings of the Japan Society* 3 (IV): 128–183.
    1902   Recent excavations at Stonehenge. *Archaeologia* 58: 37–105.

Harada, Dairoku
    1966   *The Real Existence of Myths.* 『実在した神話』 Tokyo: Gakuseisha.

Harunari, Hideji 春成秀爾
    1983   Pit burial zone. 「竪穴墓域論」 *Hokkaido Kokogaku* 19: 1–18.

Hasebe, Kotondo 長谷部言人
    1920   On flexed burial of the Stone Age. 「石器時代の蹲葬について」 *Jinruigaku Zasshi* 35 (1): 22–28.

Hayashi, Kensaku 林謙作
    1971   Burial custom of the Jomon Period, Part I: A Historical Survey. 「縄文時代の葬制、第I部 研究史」 *Kokogaku Zassi* 62 (4): 1–19.

1977a Burial custom of the Jomon Period, Part II: Arrangement of Corpus and Head Orientation, in Particular.「縄文時代の葬制、第II部：遺体の配列、とくに頭位方向」*Kokogaku Zassi* 63 (3): 1–36.

1977b Head orientation of Getenyama burials with reference to belief in after world among the Ainu.「御殿山墳墓群ノ埋葬頭位ヲ論シ併セテあいぬ族の他界観ニ及フ」*Hoppobunka Kennkyu* 11: 1–28.

Hirooka, Kimio 広岡公夫
 1976 The direction of horizontal axial lines of ancient Buddhist temples and archaeological terrestrial magnetism: the origin of magnetic compass in Japan.「古寺伽藍中軸線方位と古地磁気：日本における磁石使用の起源について」*Kokogaku Zasshi* 62 (1): 49–63.

Hojo, Yoshitaka 北條芳隆
 2017 *Orientation of Kofun and the Sun*.『古墳の方位と太陽』Tokyo: Doseisha.

Hutton, Ronald
 2013 The strange history of British archaeoastronomy. *Journal for the Study of Religion, Nature and Culture* 7 (4): 376–397.

Ishida, Mosaku 石田茂作
 1944 *A Study of Buddhist Temple Remains of the Asuka Period*.『総説飛鳥時代寺院址の研究』Tokyo: Ohtsuka Kogeisha.

Izumi, Takeshi 泉武
 2018 *Star Charts of Kitora Kofun and Takatzuzuka Kofun*.『キトラ・高松塚古墳の星宿図』Tokyo: Doseisha.

Kawaguchi, Shigekazu 川口重一
 1956 Stone arrangement of Ohyu Stone Circle.「大湯環状列石の配置」*Kyodo Bunka* 11(1): 1–4.

Kobayashi, Tatsuo (ed.) 小林達雄
 2005 *Jomon Landscape*.『縄文ランドスケープ』Tokyo: Um Promotion.

Kiyono, Kenji 清野謙次
 1946 *The Formation of Japanese Ethnic Groups*.『日本民族生成論』Tokyo: Nihon Hyoron Sha.

Kobayashi, Yoshiki and Shiho Tokuda 小林由来 徳田紫穂
 2016 *A Guide for the Sun Observation of the Jomon Period at Kanayama Stone Monuments*.『金山巨石群の「縄文」太陽観察ガイド』Tokyo: Sangokan.

Kobayashi, Yukio 小林行雄
 1961 *A Study of the Kofun Period*.『古墳時代の研究』Tokyo: Aoki Shoten.

Koganei, Seiryo 小金井良精
 1923 Burial condition of Stone Age of Japan.「日本石器時代の埋葬状態」*Jinruigaku Zasshi* 38 (1): 25–46.

Lockyer, Norman J.
 1906 *Stonehenge and Other British Stone Monuments Astronomically Considered*. London: Macmillan.

Miyajima, Kazuhiko 宮島一彦
 1999 Astronomical chart of Kitora Kofun.「キトラ古墳天文図」*Research Report of Cultural Heritage in Asuka Village: Scientific Research on*

            Kotora Kofun 『明日香村教育委員会：キトラ古墳学術調査報告書』, 51–63. Asuka Mura Kyoiku Iinkai.
   2018   Drawing styles or projection methods of the East Asian star maps and full scale restoration of the Shuiyun yixiang-tai. 「東アジアの星図作図様式と水運儀象台の原寸復元」 *RIMS Kokyuroku Bessatsu* B69: 141–150.

Morgan, Lewis H.
   1877   *Ancient Society*. London: Macmillan & Company.

Mori, Sachihiko 森幸彦
   1988   On burial condition. 「埋葬状態について」 *Sanganji Shellmound* 『三貫地貝塚』, pp. 338–352. Aizu: Fukushima Prefectural Museum.

Munro, N. Gordon
   1908   *Prehistoric Japan*. Yokohama: Johnson Reprint Corporation.
   1961   *Ainu Creed and Cult*. London: Routledge & Keegan Paul.

Nakamura, Tsukou 中村士
   2018   *Deciphering the Ancient Starry Sky from the Kitora Tumulus Star Map: A History of Star Maps and Catalogues in Asia*. 『古代の星空を読み解く：キトラ古墳天文図とアジアの星図』 Tokyo: Tokyo Daigaku Shuppan.

Nishida, Yatutami 西田泰民
   1996   Death and the Jomon Culture. 「死と縄文文化」 In: T. Izumi (ed.), *The Emergence of Jomon Pottery* 『縄文土器出現』, pp. 94–107. Tokyo: Kodansha.

Ogushi, Kikujiro 大串菊次郎
   1920   A few personal considerations on Stone Age sites, Tsugumo Shell Mound and Kou Site. 「津雲貝塚及国府石器時代遺跡に對する二三の私見」 *Rekishi to Minzoku* 3 (4): 1–34.

Ohtsuka, Kazuyoshi 大塚和義
   1967   Burial customs of the Jomon Period: a classification of burial types. 「縄文時代葬制：埋葬形態による分類」 *Shien* 27 (3): 18–41.

Okamoto, Izamu 岡本勇
   1956   Burials. 「埋葬」 In: *Lectures of Japanese Archaeology 3: the Jomon Culture* 『日本考古学講座3：縄文文化』, pp. 321–338. Tokyo: Kawade Shobo.

Sago, Tsutomu 佐合勤, Osamu Yamada, and Lyle B. Borst
   1986   Archaeoastronomical analysis of Oshoro Stone Circles in Hokkaido. *Kyoto Sangyo Daigaku Ronshu* 『京都産業大学論集：自然系列』 15: 100–115.

Saito, Kuniji 斉藤国治
   1982   *Astronomy of the Asuka Period*. 『飛鳥時代の天文学』. Tokyo: Kawade Shobo.

Saito, Tadashi 斎藤忠
   1953   On orientation of tululi. 「古墳方位考」 *Kokogaku Zasshi* 39 (2): 34–40.
   1961   *A Study of Tofun in Japan*. 『日本の古墳の研究』 Tokyo: Yoshikawa Kobunkan.

Sasaki, Chsei
    1988   A belief in souls seen from burial customs. 「埋葬状態からみた霊魂観」, In: *Sanganji Shellmound* 『三貫地貝塚』, pp. 372–379. Aizu: Fukushima Prefectural Museum [福島県立博物館].

Shichida, Tadaaki 七田忠昭
    2012   Yamatai-koku: an example of Kyushu hypothesis. 「邪馬台国：九州説の一例」 In: *Countries around Yamatai-koku (Quarterly of Archaeology, Supplement 18)* 『邪馬台国をめぐる国々』 (季刊考古学別冊18), pp. 141–148. Tokyo: Yuzankaku.

Togashi, Yasutoki 富樫泰時
    1995   「秋田大湯遺跡」 Ohyu Site, Akita Prefecture. In: T. Kobayashi (ed.), *Socialization of Nature in the Jomon Period (Quarterly of Archaeology, Supplement 6)* 『縄文時代における自然の社会化』 (季刊考古学別冊6), pp. 30–41. Tokyo: Yuzankaku.

Tshude, Hiroshi 都出比呂志
    1979   The society at the beginning period of Key-hole *tumuli*. 「前方後円墳出現期の社会」 *Kokogaku Kenkyu* 26 (3): 17–34.
    1989   The birth of Key-hole *tumuli* 「前方後円墳の誕生」 In: T. Shiraishi (ed.), *Considering the Ancient Age: the Tumuli* 『古代を考える：古墳』, pp. 1–35. Tokyo: Yoshikawa Kobunkan.

Watanabe, Makoto 渡辺誠
    1969   A few problems on burial system in the Kamegaoka Culture. 「亀ヶ岡文化をめぐる埋葬形態をめぐる二、三の問題」 *Hokuo Kodaibunka* 2: 35–44.

Watanabe, Naotsune 渡辺直経
    1959   The direction of remnant magnetism of baked earth and its application to chronology for anthropology and archaeology in Japan. *Journal of Faculty of Science, University of Tokyo* 2: 1–188.

Yamada, Yasuhiro 山田康弘
    2003   Does burial head orientation show social organization: an re-examination by Jomon skeletons. 「頭位方向は社会組織を表すのか：縄文時代の人骨出土例による再検討」 *Collection of Archaeological Papers of Ritsumeikan University* 3 (1), 341–366.

6 Fallen star legends in Japanese folk beliefs

Fallen star legends in old literature

In the oldest existing pieces of Japanese literature, the *Nihonshoki* and *Shoku-Nihongi* (*Ex-Japanese Chronicle*) 『続日本紀』, there are more than 60 instances of abnormal phenomena recorded prior to 710, when the Heijo Capital 平城京 was established in Nara. Such phenomena include eclipses, shooting stars, comets, auroras, Venus being visible during the daytime, and several others. Those phenomena were generally considered to be signs of bad fortune.

The oldest recorded abnormal phenomenon happened in 637 of Emperor Jomei's Era. The *Nihonshoki* has it that:

> A great star floated from East to West, and there was a noise like that of thunder. The people of that day said that it was the sound of the falling star. Others said that it was earth-thunder. Hereupon the Buddhist Priest Bin said: "It is not the falling star, but the Celestial Dog, the sound of whose barking is like thunder."
> (Aston 1972, Vol. 2: 167)

The celestial dog could possibly be of *tengu* 天狗 origin, which is a demon with a long nose. Further, in 639 of the same emperor's era: "a long star appeared in the northwest. Priest Bin said that it was a bosom-star. When it appeared, there was famine" (Aston 1972, Vol. 2: 169).

In 640, the star encountered the moon and this phenomenon was believed to be an omen forecasting a disaster (ibid.). Concerning this star, Aston wrote: "Chinese history records that Venus entering the moon was looked upon by the diviners as portending mortally among the people" (Aston 1972: 16), suggesting that this star was Venus. On the other hand, the astronomer Saito Kuniji argued that the star was Aldebaran and he arrived at this conclusion using an astronomical calculation (Saito 1982: 14).

In 685 of Emperor Tenmu's Era, the *Nihonshoki* states:

> On this evening at twilight, a great star passed from the East to the West ... A thing appeared in shape like a Buddhist baptismal flag and was of a flame color. It floated through the void towards the north and was seen by all the provinces. Some said it sank into the Sea of Koshi. On this day a white vapor arose on the Eastern Mountain, four fathoms in size.
>
> (Aston 1972, Vol. 2: 357)

Here, Koshi 越 refers to present-day Niigata Prefecture, which lies northeast of Yamato, facing the Japan Sea.

In addition, the *Fudoki* 『風土記』 states: There was a stone in Mt. Tamaoki of Owari County 尾張 (Aichi Prefecture). It was where a red star fell and there lies a *hoshi-ike* (star pond) at its foot. The water of the pond always mirrors a star and a star lives in the pond. There is a strange rock that was considered to be a transformation of a star and even today stars fall on the mountain from time to time.

Additionally, in a report from Iyo County 伊予 (Ehime Prefecture), it is written that: A mountain in heaven was divided and fell onto earth. One became Mt. Tenzan in Iyo County and another became Mt. Ameno-Kaguyama 天香久山 in Yamato County 大和 (Nara Prefecture).

In this way, unusual astronomical phenomena (fallen stars in particular) were often recognized as ominous signs. But in western Japan, there are several Shinto shrines that worship the remnants of fallen stars as a sacred object (Figure 6.1).

Shrines of fallen star legend: Kudamatsu of Yamaguchi Prefecture

One of the most famous examples of fallen star legends came from Kudamatsu 下松 of Yamaguchi Prefecture (Figure 6.1: 4). On September 18, 595, a large star descended upon a pine tree of Aoyanagi-ura Beach, which is now in Kudamatsu City. The star illuminated for seven nights like a full moon. An augur said: "I am the bodhisattva Myoken. After three months and three days, Prince Rinsho 琳聖太子 of the Paekche Kingdom 百済 of Korea will come here. Tell Prince Shotoku 聖徳太子 to welcome him to Japan" (Sugihara 1985: 23–25).

Legend has that it was then, when Prince Rinsho actually came to Kudamatsu, that Prince Shotoku sent Hata Kwakatsu 秦川勝 to see him. It is also said that Prince Rinsho introduced star-worship rituals, in particular, those of Myoken, to Japan for the first time in 597 (Ueno 2010: 138).

Fallen star legends in folk beliefs 91

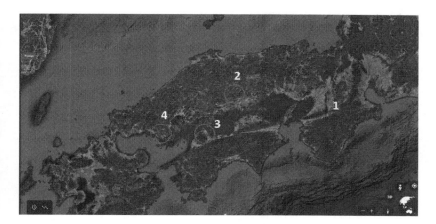

Figure 6.1 Map of western Japan.
Notes
1 Katano and Hirakata City Area (Osaka).
2 Okayama City and Bisei Town Area (Okayama).
3 Imabari City and Nihama City Area (Ehime).
4 Kudamatsu Town Area (Yamaguchi).

At the place where pine trees were standing, now lies Kanawa Shrine 金輪神社. Three pine trees used to stand at that time and these trees were named "pine trees shaped like a tripod kettle" (Figure 6.2: a).

Prince Rinsho departed to Japan and landed on Tatara Beach near Kudamatsu. Price Rinsho built a palace on Mt. Juto 鷲頭山 where he established a star shrine to worship the Bodhisattva Myoken. This shrine is now the Kudamatsu Shrine (Figure 6.2: b), but because of the separation between gods and Buddha 神仏分離令 in the Meiji Era (after 1868), Myoken has moved to the Buddhist Juto Temple (Sugihara 1985) (Figure 6.2: c).

Descendants of Prince Rinsho became the Tatara Clan 多々良氏, which later changed into the Ouchi Clan 大内氏. The Ouchi Clan governed this area from the Medieval Period until the fifteenth century. Many historians consider that the legend of Prince Rinsho was fiction for several reasons. Probably the Ouchi Clan created this legend to legitimate their origin as descending from Korean nobles (Kudamatsu Shishi Hensan Iinkai 1989).

I do not discuss the validity of such legends here. The point is that the Prince Rinsho was said to be the ancestor of the Tatara Clan. *Tatara* originally means cupola furnace or foot-operated bellows and the term later came to mean specialists of forging and iron-making. This place was famous for forging by sand iron and the Ouchi Clan was also known to

92 *Fallen star legends in folk beliefs*

(a)

(b)

(c)

Figure 6.2 Shrines and Temples in Kudamatsu City related to fallen star legends.
Notes
a Kanawa Jinja and the Pine Tree.
b Kudamatsu Shrine.
c Jutosan Temple.

have been active in developing mines (e.g., *Iwami* Silver Mine) (Wakao 1980: 124). The important point here is that the fallen star legend was closely related to the introduction of advanced forging technology and star worship from the Asian continent.

Hoshida Shrine in Katano City, Osaka

This legend is closely related to the famous monk Kobodaishi 弘法大師 or Kukai 空海. Kukai is the founder of Esoteric Buddhism and astrology, which was brought from China. He is also considered to have been actively engaged in developing mines.

In the early ninth century, legend has it that Kukai was training and chanting a mantra in a cave of Katano City (Figure 6.1: 1). Then from heaven, a large star fell and broke into three pieces. One fragment fell in an area called *hoshi-no-mori* 星の森 ("forest of stars"), one fell on Korinji Temple 光林寺 (Figure 6.3: a), and the last one fell on the summit of Mt. Hoshida Myoken 星田妙見 (*hoshida* meaning "field of stars"). The rock in the yard of Korinji Temple is said to be the remnant of the fallen star (Figure 6.3: b). Interestingly, these three places form an equilateral triangle (Akiyama 2008).

Presently, Hoshida Myoken Shrine exists on the summit of Mt. Hoshida Myoken (Figure 6.3: c). Behind the shrine on the summit, there is a rock that is said to be the remnants of the fallen star at that time (Figure 6.3: d).

In Neyagawa City, just west of Hoshida Myoken Shrine, there are place names that remind us of the Hata Clan: Hata, Uzumasa, and Kawakatsu. The Hata Clan are considered to be specialists responsible for flood control. In Neyagawa City, there is Hosoya Shrine 細谷神社, but in historic records preserved in one of town's old family Nishijima, that shrine was originally the Hoshiya Shrine 星谷神社, which means "Star Shrine." Ueno believes that this shrine was established by the Hata Clan from China and worshiped stars on the basis of Chinese star customs (Ueno 2010: 131–134).

Hata Kawakatsu, who was said to have welcomed Prince Rinsho at Kudamatsu, was living in the Neyagawa area. This area had strategic importance in water transportation between Setouchi Inland Sea, Osaka Basin, and the capital in Nara. Ueno pointed out that the Hoshida Myoken Shrine was located to observe north, south, and west in order to control the water transport of the Yodogawa water system (Ueno 2010).

The Hata Clan were originally seafarers to whom the Polaris was important, probably as a guiding star of navigation. Myoken symbolizes the Polar Star whose worship is considered to have been spread by the Hata Clan.

94 *Fallen star legends in folk beliefs*

Figure 6.3 Monuments, Shrines, and Temples in Katano City related to fallen star legends.

Notes
a Korinji Temple.
b The rock said to be the remnant of a fallen star.
c Hoshida Myoken Shrine.
d The rock said to be the remnant of a fallen star.

Kibi Region, Okayama Prefecture

Bisei Town, now included in present-day Ihara City, is located in a mountainous area in Okayama Prefecture (Figure 6.1: 2). There is a legend about the origin of three shrines in the area that originated from a fallen star (Bisei Choshi Hensan Iinkai 1976).

In early the twelfth century, three shooting stars fell to the earth. The local chief who governed this area built a small shrine to worship the stars. When his descendants became ill, he prayed to the stars. One night he dreamed of Hoshio 星尾, one of the 28 *Sei Shuku* (Chinese lunar houses), and he recovered. Then he rebuilt the previous small shrine into Hoshio Jinja 星尾神社, which means "star tail shrine" (Figure 6.4: a).

Originally this shrine was facing south. When the fishing catch continued to be poor, fishermen heard an oracle that they should face the

Fallen star legends in folk beliefs 95

(a)

(b)

(c)

Figure 6.4 Shrines and Temples related to fallen star legend in Bisei Towan.
Notes
a   Hoshio Shrine.
b   Takaboshi Shrine.
c   Myojin-sha Temple.

shrine to the north, which is the direction of Myoken. Until the beginning of the twentieth century, fishermen used to visit the shrine to ensure a good catch.

The other two shrines from this story are Takaboshi Jinja 高星神社, meaning "high star" (Figure 6.4: b), and Myojinsha 明神社 meaning "bright star" (Figure 6.4: c).

A similar legend is recorded about the Hoshi Shrine 星神社 of the Manaboshi Area of northern Okayama City. Legend has it that during the era of Emperor Tenmu (673–686), a black cloud suddenly descended, and thunder continued for 31 days. The people did not go near the mountain out of fear and they saw something shining on the mountain summit. When they asked an *omnyoji* 陰陽師 (an astrologer) to divine it, the *onmyoji* said that three rocks fell on the summit, and it was a symptom that Mikahaka-Hikono-Mikoto descended from heaven to the earth.

Mika means "round object," as discussed in the previous chapter concerning Ama-tsu-mika-hoshi, and the name of the god who descended might be its variant. The villagers constructed a shrine and changed the place name to Mana-boshi 真星 ("true star"). Three rocks behind the shrine are believed to be those that fell from heaven (Figure 6.5).

In the Shimori District where the shrine is located, there is a place called Kami-Hata Village (Upper Hata) 上土田村 and "hata" refers to the Hata Clan who is said to have migrated to here. There is also a place named Ohnaru 大成, which could be derived from the site of smoked iron (Okayama City Society for the Study of Place Names 1989).

This area is part of the ancient Kibi Kingdom that was once a competing hegemony with the Yamato Kingdom. The reason why Kibi was so strong politically was that this area was the center of most advanced iron forging at that age. This area is famous for iron sand and archaeological evidence shows that the iron-making technology introduced from the Korean Peninsula was innovated considerably in this area.

Iyo County (Ehime Prefecture)

In Iyo Country (Ehime Prefecture) of Shikoku Island, there are shrines constructed on the basis of fallen star legends (Figure 6.1: 3). These include Hoshi Jinja (star shrine) located in the Hoshi Ura (star inlet) 星浦 in Onishi Town (Figure 6.6: a) and Manaboshi Jinja (true star shrine) in Hoshihara (star field) of Nihama Town (Figure 6.6: b).

The place in Iyo County where these shrines are located is known for being rich in mineral resources. One of the biggest copper mines in Japan, Besshi Copper Mine 別子銅山, is located here. This area is famous for mercury. Mercury was important for decorating Buddha Statues in the

Fallen star legends in folk beliefs 97

(a)

(b)

(c)

Figure 6.5 Hoshi Jinja Shrine in Okayama City.
Notes
a   Hoshi Jinja Shrine.
b   The Emblem symbolizing fallen star cracked in to three parts.
c   Sacred Rocks said to be cracked fallen star.

98 *Fallen star legends in folk beliefs*

(a)

(b)

Figure 6.6 Shrines related to fallen star legends in Imabari City and Nihama City.
Notes
a Hoshi Jinja Shrine, Imabari.
b Manaboshi Jinja Shrine, Nihama.

capital. In addition, this area is known as the place where the Hata Clan actively engaged in trading, mining, and probably forging mercury. I would add that this area was the home base of the monk Kukai, who had a strong relationship with the Hata Clan, star worship, and probably mining as well.

The following example has been recorded in Japanese folklore. About 600 years ago in Iyo, in Onishi Town (now belonging to Imabari City), there is a legend saying that a star fell in this area. Since it was a curious stone, children played with the stone by rolling it. Adults, seeing this, warned against this as it might induce bad karma. Then a serious disease spread among the population and the people constructed the Hoshi Jinja (star shrine) for worshiping the stone. They named this area as Hoshi Ura (star inlet) (Nishioka 1976: 82–83).

In Nihama City, east of Onishi Town, there is another star shrine, which is the Manaboshi (real star) Shrine at Hoshibara (star field). According to historical records, a meteorite once fell in this area and the villagers constructed the shrine to worship it. The shrine still prohibits ordinary people to see the sacred object.

In the Heian Era (794–1192), during the days of the annual festival, from July 14 to 26, and from December 14 to 28, a market was opened in this shrine. Those days of the old calendar correspond to summer solstice and winter solstice respectively (Nihama Shishi Hensan Iinkai 1980).

Discussion

Japanese star worship is complex, as it is syncretized with Kokuzo-Bosatsu worship 虚空蔵菩薩 (Bodhisattva Akasagarbha) and Esoteric Buddhism (Sano 1994). It was Kuka who introduced Esoteric Buddhism, including star worship from the Tang Dynasty of China, to Japan during the early ninth century. He is also considered to have been ambitious in developing the area's mining industry. The temples of the Shingon Mission 真言宗, founded by Kukai, were often built in mountains near mines (Tani 1983; Sato 1991).

In relation to this, historians and folklorists have noticed the close relationship between star worship and mine developers (Sato et al. 1991; Wakao 1994). Historical records indicate that pioneer miners were immigrants from Korea and the northern Kanto region (north of Tokyo), and that they constructed many star shrines near mines. Among these naturalized Japanese, the Hata Clan was most known.

Mine developers tend to worship the Bodhisattva Myoken, symbolized as the Polar Star and believe that mineral resources originated from heaven (Ohwa 2013: 370; Tani 1983). Among *tatara*, iron forgers, belief in

Kanayako-gami 金屋子神 is popular. This is the belief that forgers descended from heaven onto the mountain and started making iron. They had strong taboos, such as the taboo of touching women (Inada et al. 1994: 545). The relevance of Myoken belief to ironwork is also pointed out among samurai clans of the Boso Peninsula 房総半島 and the Chiba Clan 千葉氏 (Marui 2013).

There are many Hoshi Jinja 星神社 (star shrines) in the northern Kanto region. Most of them enshrine gods of Iwasaku 岩裂 (rock-splitting god) and Nesaku 根裂 (root-splitting gods). In Ancient myths (see Chapter 2), when the goddess Izanami was delivering babies, she died because her genitals were burned by the fire god Kagutsuchi 迦具土神. Izanaki felt sorry for Izanami and felt angry about the fire god, and, in response, he cut Kagutsuchi into three pieces, each of which became a god. One version of the *Nihonshoki* states that the blood that dripped from the edge of the sword became the myriad of rocks which lie in the bed of Amano Yasukawara 天安河原, the Easy River of Heaven (Aston 1972: Vol. 1: 23).

Masayuki Tsugita, who translated the original text of the *Kojiki* into modern Japanese, argued that the shedding of Kaguttsuchi's blood from which several gods were transformed, reminds us of forging in which iron is burned and stroked, producing red sparks, and finally forming an iron sword (Tsugita 1977 Vol. 1: 59)

Aston argued that Amano Yasukawara represents the Milky Way and therefore the gods of Iwa-saku and Ne-saku thus formed a symbolized myriad of stars in the Milky Way (Wakao 1994: 77). Iwa-saku and Ne-saku are often worshiped in star shrines of northern Kanto and are often syncretized with Kokuzo-Bosatsu. The northern Kanto region is rich in mines and Hoshi Jinja shrines are considered to be closely related to the mining industry (Wakao 1980) and naturalized Japanese (Kurabe 1983). I argue that the act of cutting the fire god Kagutshuchi into three pieces, and the name Iwa-saku (splitting rock), have symbolic associations with forging and meteorite.

It is Mircea Eliade who recognized the relationship of meteorites to forging. He wrote,

> they [meteorites] fall to earth charged with celestial sanctity; in a way, they represent heaven. This would suggest why so many meteorites were worshiped or identified with a deity. The faithful saw in them the "first form," the immediate manifestation of the godhead.
>
> (Eliade 1956: 20)

The meteorite is associated with fire or sparks, as are blacksmiths. In New South Wales of Australia, meteors were associated with fire and linked to the *waratah* plant (*Telopea speciosissima*), whose brilliant red flowers seemed to the Aborigines like sparks from a fire. In the early years of white settlement, some Aborigines brought *waratah* flowers to the European blacksmiths. They identified the sparks from anvil with the sparks from meteors and hence with the *waratah* flower (Haynes 2000: 85–86).

In conclusion, like many groups in the world, the ancient Japanese came to believe that new technology, producing fire or sparks, or which transform stone or sand into metal, was a magical or esoteric procedure. This is especially true of the western part of Japan, which had a direct influence on cultures from the continent. This situation served to develop star worship, and fallen star legends in particular, which are associated with *kikajin* (the naturalizeded Japanese) expert group.

References

Akiyama, Kojo 秋山幸三
    2008   Materials related to Yin and Yang theory in Northern Kawachi and Hoshida Myoken-gu Shrine. 「北河内 星田妙見宮の陰陽道関係資料」 *Research Report of Osaka Prefectural Cultural Assets Center* 『大阪府文化財センター 研究報告』 6: 13–167.

Aston W.G.
    1972   *Nihongi: Chronicle of Japan from the Earliest Times to A.D. 697.* Tokyo: Tuttle.

Bisei Choshi Hensan Iinkai [Bisei Town History Editorial Board] 美星町史編集委員会
    1976   *History of Bisei Town, Okayama Prefecture.* 『岡山県 美星町史 : 通史編』、 Bisei: Bisei Town Hall.

Eliade, Mircea
    1962   *The Forge and the Crucible.* Chicago: The University of Chicago Press.

Haynes, Roslynn
    2000   Dreaming the stars. *Earth Song Journal Spring* 11: 5–12.

Inada, Koji, Takehiko Ohshima, Toyohiko Kawabata, Akira Fukuda, and Yukihisa Mihara (eds.) 稲田浩二 大島建彦 川崎豊彦 福田晃 三原幸久 (編)
    1994   *The Encyclopedia of Japanese Folktales.* 『日本昔話事典』 Tokyo: Kobundo.

Kudamatsu Shishi Hensan Iinkai [Kudamatsu City History Editorial Board] 下松市史 編纂委員会
    1989   *History of Kudamatsu City.* 『下松市史 : 通史編』 Kudamatsu: Kudakmatsu City Hall.

Kurabe, Masato 倉部真人
    1983   Mining industry groups and the worship of Star Shrine. 「金属採鉱者

集団と 「星の宮」信仰 Higashi-Ajiano Kodai Bunka 『東アジアの古代文化』35: 156–162.

Marui, Keiji 丸井敬司
    2013   *Chiba Clan and Myoken Belief.* 『千葉氏と妙見信仰』Tokyo: Iwata Shoin.

Nihama Shishi Hensan Iinkai [Nihama City History Editorial Board] 新居浜市史編纂 委員会
    1980   *History of Niham City* 『新居浜市史』Nihama: Nihama City Hall.

Nishioka, Chizu 西岡千頭
    1976   A Story of Stars and Cosmos. 『星と宇宙の話』Matsuyama: Ehime Bunka Sosho.

Ohwa, Iwao 大和岩雄
    2013   *More on the Study of Hata Clan.* 『続 秦氏の研究』Tokyo: Daiwa Shobo.

Okayama City Society for the Study of Place Names 岡山市地名研究会
    1989   *Place Names of Okayama City.* 『岡山市の地名』、Tokyo: Kadokawa Shoten.

Saito, Kuniji 斉藤国治
    1982   *Astronomy of the Asuka Period.* 『飛鳥時代の天文学』. Tokyo: Kawade Shobo.

Sano, Kenji 佐野賢治
    1994   An introduction to the history of worship of star gods in Japan: focused on Myoken and Kokuzo Botatsu beliefs. 「日本神星信仰史概論： 妙見 虚空蔵信仰 を中心にして」 In: K. Sano (ed.), *Belief of Stars: Myoken and Kokuzo* 『星の 信仰： 妙見 虚空蔵』, pp. 3–53. Tokyo: Keisuisha.

Sato, Tamotsu 佐藤任
    1991   *Kukai and Alchemy: A Consideration based on Metallurgy History.* 『空海と錬金術：金属史観による考察』Tokyo: Tokyo Shoseki.

Sato, Tamotsu, Junji Horii, Seiichi Honjo, Shinichi Yuki, and Ituso Wakao 佐藤任 堀井 順次 本城清一 柚木伸一 若尾五雄
    1991   *Shingon Esoteric Buddhism and Ancient Metal Culture.* 『真言密教と古代金属 文化』Ohsaka: Toyo Shuppan.

Sugihara, Takatoshi 杉原孝俊
    1985   *Myoken.* 『妙見さま』Kudamatsu: Myokengu Shutoji Temple.

Tani, Yuji 谷有二
    1983   *The Enigma of Mountain Lore of Japan.* 『日本山岳伝承の謎』Tokyo: Miraisha.

Tsugita, Masaki 次田真幸
    1977   *Kojiki*, 3 Volumes. 『古事記』Tokyo: Kodansha.

Ueno, Kanako 植野加代子
    2010   *Hata Clan and Myoken Belief.* 『秦氏と妙見信仰』Tokyo: Iwata Shoin.

Wakao, Itsuo 若尾五雄
    1980   Mines and belief. 「鉱山と信仰」 *Rekishi-Koron* 『歴史公論』56: 123–130.
    1994   *Gold and Centipede: The Road to Mine Folklore.* 『黄金と百足』Tokyo: Jinbun Shoin..

7 Cosmology seen in house and burial orientation of the Hokkaido Ainu, northern Japan

The orientations of houses and burials seem to have been decided based on several factors, such as river orientation, land slope, and various others. Ainu villages were typically arranged along a river and the river's upstream movement toward a sacred mountain was just as important as the eastward orientation. I will examine whether this difference came from regional or temporal variation.

Prehistoric chronology in Hokkaido

The prehistoric chronology of Japan is shown in Figure 7.2. In Hokkaido, where rice cultivation was then impossible, a distinct Post-Jomon culture

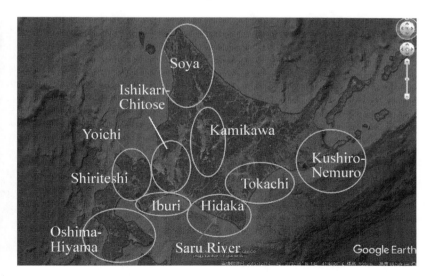

Figure 7.1 Hokkaido and its regions mentioned in this chapter.

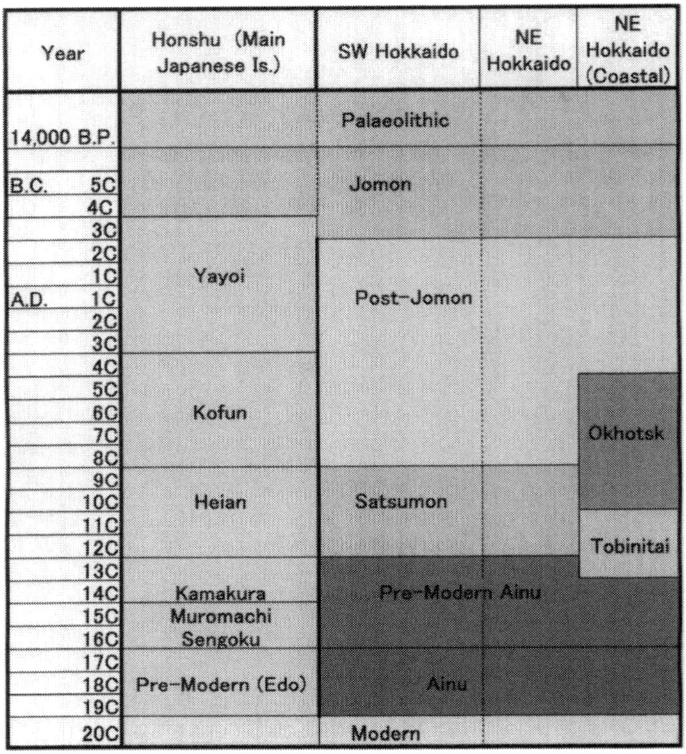

Year	Honshu (Main Japanese Is.)	SW Hokkaido	NE Hokkaido	NE Hokkaido (Coastal)
14,000 B.P.		Palaeolithic		
B.C. 5C		Jomon		
4C				
3C				
2C				
1C	Yayoi			
A.D. 1C		Post-Jomon		
2C				
3C				
4C				
5C				
6C	Kofun			
7C				Okhotsk
8C				
9C				
10C	Heian	Satsumon		
11C				
12C				Tobinitai
13C				
14C	Kamakura	Pre-Modern Ainu		
15C	Muromachi			
16C	Sengoku			
17C				
18C	Pre-Modern (Edo)	Ainu		
19C				
20C		Modern		

Figure 7.2 Prehistoric chronology of Hokkaido and Honshu (Japan's main island).

succeeded the Jomon Period and a foraging economy persisted. After the development of Post-Jomon culture (until third century BCE), the societies inland and in southwestern Hokkaido developed into what has come to be called Satsumon culture (third century BCE to seventh century CE), which is considered the direct ancestor of the Hokkaido Ainu culture today. In contrast, northeast Hokkaido, especially the coastal zone of Okhotsk Sea, was settled by the people practicing the Okhotsk culture (third to thirteenth century CE), which originated in Southern Sakhalin. The Okhotsk culture was a maritime culture characterized by sea mammal hunting, fishing, and sea trading, and contributed significantly to introducing civilization-derived valuables, such as glass beads and metal ornaments, to Hokkaido.

At some point, northeast Hokkaido developed a creole culture, which blended elements from both Okhotsk and Satsumon cultures, and which is referred to as Tobinitai culture (ninth to thirteenth century CE). Thereafter, the Satsumon culture, absorbing the Tobinitai culture, changed into what is now referred to as Ainu culture throughout Hokkaido. However, regional differences before the emergence of Ainu culture are an important factor, among others, that has led to regional variation within the Hokkaido Ainu.

Life and settlement of the Hokkaido Ainu

Ainu society was structured around nuclear families and each family lived a house called a *chise* (Ainu Culture Preservation Council 1969). *Chise* contain one rectangular room and an entrance chamber was often attached to the side (Figure 7.3: a, b). In the middle of the room there was a hearth

(a)

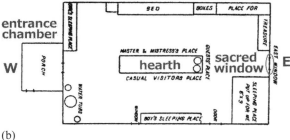
(b)

Figure 7.3 Ainu House (chise).

Notes
a Exhibited Ainu house at the Kayano Shigeru Ainu Museum in Biratori Town.
b Inner structure of the Ainu house (modified from Batchelor 1927: 67).

and at the end of the house's long axis, families created a sacred window known as *rorun-puyar* (or *kamuy puyara*, "window of gods"). It was believed that only gods could enter through the sacred window and it was considered very impolite to look into other people's houses through this window (Batchelor 1927: 171–172). A sacred altar was situated outside this window (Ainu Culture Preservation Council 1969).

The *iomante* (meaning "to send or dedicate to gods") was the most important ceremony for the Ainu (Kadosaski 2016). The *iomante* is a ritual for sending the souls of hunted animals to the world of the gods. This ritual was applied not only to bears but also to other animals, such as foxes, raccoon dogs, and owls, among others (Utagawa 2004a). Bear *iomante* were the most important to the Ainu and thus this term is often translated as "bear ceremony."

The Ainu hunted bears in hibernation during February and captured baby bears. The captured baby bears were traditionally brought back to villages and raised in pens. Ainu husbands could watch the pen from inside of the house through the sacred window.

When the bear turned two or three years old, around December solstice of that year, the bear was ritually killed in order to return it to the world of the gods, *kamuy mosir* (*kamuy* [god], *mosir* [world]). The skull of the killed bear was to be brought into the house through the sacred window. The skull was beautifully decorated and offered many foods. The baby bear was thus treated with great hospitality and would tell gods in *kamuy mosir* that the human world was a good place to visit. The completion of this ritual means that a good hunting season was promised in the following year since the bear is considered to be king of the animal world.

Indigenous orientation system

In the Ainu language, there are many words that describe the sun and among them *cup-kamuy* (*cup* [constellation or round light object], *kamuy* [god]) or *tokap-cup-kamuy* (*tokap* [bright]) are used most widely. The gender of the sun was either male or female, but in *Yūkara*, an Ainu epic poem, the sun is usually considered to be male. The word for road is *ru* and there is a called concept *cup-ru* (road of the sun), which corresponds to the ecliptic in astronomy.

The Ainu had an orientation system based on the movement of the sun (*cup*) (Sueoka 2009: 32). The east is recognized as the direction of the sunrise, *cup-ka* (*ka* [rise]), and west as the direction of the sunset, *cup-pok* (*pok* [set]). In the east, they recognized three points corresponding to the rising point of the sun: summer solstice, equinox, and winter solstice. In the same way, three points are recognized in the west, corresponding to the sun setting point on solstices and equinox. They were called as follows:

cupketok (*cupka* [sunrise] + *etok* [head])	=	Summer Solstice sunrise Point
cuppoketok (*cuppok* [sunset] + *etok*)	=	Summer Solstice sunset Point
cupkarantom (*cupka* + *rantom* [middle])	=	Equinox sunrise Point
cuppokramtom (*cuppok* + *rantom*)	=	Exuinox sunset Point
cupko (*cupka* + *o* [*hip*])	=	Winter Solstice sunrise Point
cuppoko (*cuppk* + *o*)	=	Winter Solstice sunset Point

There is evidence that the Ainu observed the seasonal movement of the sun from a certain spot in each village and that they constructed a wooden frame to measure the movement of the sun. This spot was called *inukarni* (*i* [it or the sun], *nukar* [to observe], *ni* [wood]) (Sueoka 2009: 33).

The period when the sun is moving to the left (north) from *cupkarantom* (equinox point) is called *paykar* (*pa* [year], *e* [there], *kar* [make]), which corresponds to spring; the period when the sun is moving back to the right (south) from the northern end, *cupketok* (summer solstice point) is *sak*, and corresponds to summer; the period when the sun, is moving further right (south) passing the *cupketok* corresponds to autumn, *cuk* (to wither); and the period when the sun is moving back to the left (north) from the right end, *cupko* (winter solstice point), corresponds to winter, *mata* (Sueoka 2009: 44).

The ritual *sinnorappa* (to weep) or *iacrapa* (to give or dedicate) was practiced to worship ancestral spirits and these rituals were probably held around summer solstice. In addition, the Ainu seem to have had seasonal rituals performed during vernal and autumnal equinoxes.

In addition to the east-west orientation, the Ainu had several types of indigenous orientation used for daily life (Sueoka 1979: 36). Interestingly, Polaris was not so important to the Ainu and only the Ainu of northern and central Hokkaido had a name for Polar Star, *poro nociw*, which means "a great star" (Sueoka 1979, 2009). It seems that in the everyday life of the Ainu, cardinal orientation was not as important as a more practical one explained below.

For practical orientation, the most important concept was the contrast of upriver and downriver, since Ainu villages were usually situated along rivers. The upriver direction was especially important for the Ainu because this direction usually corresponded to the direction of the sacred mountain where gods and ancestors were said to live (Watanabe 1990).

Another practical orientation is concerned with the contrast of seaward vs. landward. This is similar to other societies that lived in island conditions, such as the Polynesians. In the Ainu language, mountain is *kimun*

108 *Cosmology in house and burial orientation*

and open sea is *pisun* or *repun*, and *e kimun* means "to the mountain" and *o kimun* means "from the mountain." In a similar way, *e pisun* (or *repun*) means "to the sea" and *o pisun* (or *repun*) means "from the sea."

In addition, the Ainu use *pa*, meaning both "a head" and "open sea," and *kes*, meaning both "a hip" and "inland." If the shoreline runs from north to south, and the land lies in the west, *pa* indicates the east and *kes* indicates the west. If the shoreline runs from east to west, and the land lies in the north, *pa* indicates the south and *kes* indicates the north.

The hunting territory of the Ainu, *iwor*, is divided into *sanke iwor*, "close hunting ground" (*sanke* [close]), *makun iwor*, "hunting ground in the back" (*mak* [back], *un* [to be], *iwor*), *kimun iwor*, "mountain hunting ground" (*kim* [mountain]), and *mosir utur*, "beyond country border" (*mosir* [country], *utur* [border]). In addition to these, there are more conceptual categories, *pekercupkamuy*, "good god of the sun," (*pekere* [bright], *cup* [sun], *kamuy* [god]) where the sun rises, and *wenkamuy*, "bad god's territory," (*wen* [bad]) where the sun sets.

Wen kamuy lies as far as they could imagine and it is where souls ultimately went after dying. Where *nis* (heaven) crosses the *cupru* (the road of the sun), there are rising and setting points of the sun, where gods like *pekerkamuy* or *pekercupkamuy* live. Under the point where the sun sets lies *pokna mosir*, the afterworld (*pokna* [under earth]), which is the world of the dead.

Dwelling structure and the sacred window

Several possibilities have been proposed concerning the orientation of Ainu houses: (1) east (sunrise direction), (2) upriver, or (3) sacred mountain. For instance, in the Chitose River Basin in southwestern Hokkaido, there is a strong tendency for the sacred window to be directed toward the east, although in this region the sacred mountain is located in the west. There is an oral history that says the Ainu people introduced the light of sunrise through this window and one informant stated that they should avoid facing the sacred window toward the sacred mountain (often lying upriver direction) since it is impolite to the gods (Matsui 1999: 52).

Among excavated houses belonging to the Pre-Modern Ainu Period compiled by Kobayashi (Kobayashi 2010), 24 samples have an entrance chamber (Figure 7.5). If we assume that the sacred window is situated on the opposite side of the house along the long axis, all the 24 examples demonstrate an orientation belonging to the eastern half of the horizon (35–130 degrees).

At the Karinba 1 Site of Eniwa City in the Chitose Basin, ten houses were excavated (Figure 7.4: 1) (Eniwa City Board of Education, 2005,

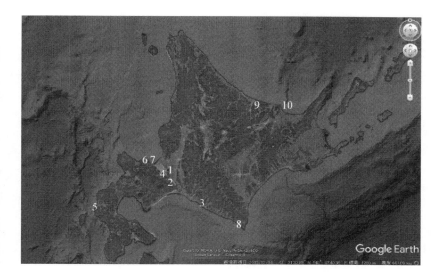

Figure 7.4 Archaeological sites mentioned in this chapter.
Notes
1: Karinba, 2: Iruekashi, 3: Suehiro. 4: Usakumai, 5: Minamikawa,
6: Irifune, 7: Ukai-chiten, 8: Shinhama, 9: Motomonbetsu, 10: Moyoro.

Fig. 53). Among them, three houses have an entrance chamber on the western side, so the sacred windows must have been facing the eastern side (Figure 7.6). We can assume that the sacred windows of other houses without entrance chambers were also located on the eastern side of houses.

At the Iruekashi Site of Biratori Town (Figure 7.4: 2), ten houses were also excavated. No entrance chamber is found in these houses, but if we assume that the sacred window is located along the long axis, then the sacred windows were facing either northeast or southwest. Even if sacred windows were facing the eastern side as ethnographic information in this town indicates (e.g., Batchelor 1927: 171), this creates another problem, since the northeast is also the direction of upriver (Uchiyama 2007).

The eastern orientation of the sacred window in the Chitose Region (and also found as far as the Hidaka Region), however, does not match the ethnographic information collected in northeastern Hokkaido (e.g., Tokachi Basin), since sacred windows there could be facing north, west, or even south (Uchida 1998) (Figure 7.7).

110 Cosmology in house and burial orientation

Figure 7.5 Estimated orientation of the sacred window in house sites with an entrance chamber.

Note
Lines SSR/WWS and SSS/WSR indicate the sunrise and sunset points at solstices.

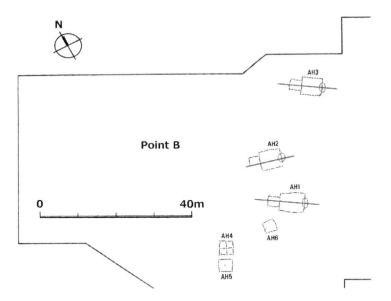

Figure 7.6 House sites with an entrance chamber in Karinba 3 site.

Source: modified from Eniwa City Board of Education 2005, Fig. 53.

Note
Solid lines through AH1, AH2 and AH3 indicate a long axis of each house and circles indicate the estimated sacred window.

Cosmology in house and burial orientation 111

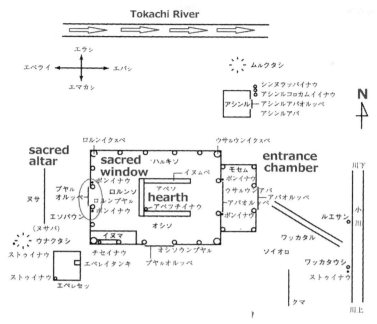

Figure 7.7 Ethnographic example of Tokachi Ainu House.
Source: modified from Uchida 1998, Fig. 1.1.

The most recent research, conducted by the Hokkaido government during the 1980s, shows that the sacred window tended to be directed to the north in eastern Hokkaido, whereas it was directed to the east in the Chitose Basin and Usu-Ugawa in the Iburi Region in southwestern Hokkaido (Hokkaido Cultural Property Preservation Office 1989, 1990). One informant in Kushiro (eastern Hokkaido) said that the sacred window was located on the southern side of the house since the south is where there is always the sun (Hokkaido Board of Education 1986: 97). There are other informants who said that the sacred window was located on the western side (Hokkaido Board of Education 1987: 58).

It is interesting to note that the Ainu in the southwest understand that the sacred window is located toward the east since it is the direction of the sun or sunrise. They even have a belief that they should avoid the direction of the sacred mountain (west) since it is impolite to the gods. In contrast, the informants in eastern areas believe that the sacred window should face south since the sun is always visible there. The last opinion is understandable because facing the window toward the south is the most practical way to receive as much sunlight as possible. Although the direction of the sacred window was often decided according to the direction of sun, the reasoning behind its actual orientation is variable even among the Ainu.

The afterworld and burial markers

There are diverse opinions among the Ainu concerning the direction of the afterworld. Some Ainu groups believe the afterworld lies in the direction of the sunset, some believe it lies upriver, others believe toward the sacred mountain, and some even believe it lies in the sea. In some areas, the entrance to the afterworld, *ahun poru*, is identified in particular caves and could be located on the coasts or in the mountains (Fujimoto 1971: 74). In addition, there was a difference between the place where the dead stayed temporarily (*pokna mosir*) and the afterword, where they finally reached (*teine pokna mosir*) (Hayashi 1977: 13–14). The place where the dead stayed was believed to be in concrete geographical features, but the afterworld was an abstract concept that could not be identified with a specific direction or location. Since the direction or location of the afterworld is far from being conclusive (e.g., Fujimura 1985; Hayashi 1977; Uchiyama 2005), I do not discuss this problem in this book.

Ainu funeral customs demonstrated regional variation similar to those found in dwelling structures. The Ainu usually place a pole on the head of the buried persons as a grave marker. It is said that the pole was used by the dead when they woke and that they could use the pole as a stick for walking into another world. The shape of burial poles differs between men and women.

Archaeologist Kono Hiromichi analyzed burial pole types and summarized their distribution, according to Ainu local groups (Kono 1932): West Endiu (Southern Sakhalin and Yoichi on the Japan Sea Coast of southwestern Hokkaido), Sum-un-kur (from Ishikari-Chitose Region to the Japan Sea Coast; *sum* [west wind]), Peni-un-kur (Central Hokkaido), Sar-un-kur (from Saru River Basin to Iburi Region, and also Chitose Basin), Menas-un-kur (eastern Hokkaido: *menas* means "east or south wind") (see Figure 7.1 for the location of regions).

Male poles tend to be shaped like an arrow or sword, or Y-shape (probably to signify a boat paddle handle or hoe). The male poles had head decorations that were distributed in the Sum-un-kur region and is shaped like the head of a sword, but the arrow-shaped with a hole is found in Sar-un-kur region. The Y-shaped type distributed exists in Menas-un-kur region in eastern Hokkaido, but this type penetrated into the Saru River Basin and co-existed with the Mar-un-kur type.

Female pole heads were either pointed with a hole, T-shaped with holes at both ends, or shaped like a bead (Kono 1931; Kubodera 2001). The

T-shaped type is distributed mainly in the Menas-un-kur region. In the Sar-un-kur region, women's poles are a straight shape with a hole, like that of a sewing needle. In the West Endiu region, female poles were shaped like a curved T-shape (signifying a bead) or a sewing needle (Kubodera 2001: 160–163).

Sueoka has pointed out that the X shape often grooved on the grave poles symbolized the Big Dipper since the Soya Ainu of northern Hokkaido called the circumpolar movement of Big Dipper *supne-nociw* (*supne* [swirling], star) or *utaspanukar-keta* (*utaspa* [facing], *nukar* [to watch each other], star). Thus, the movement of Big Dipper was imaged as X or 卍 shape (Sueoka 2009: 213–218).

Burial orientation

Past researchers have also pointed out differences in burial orientation (Fujimoto 1971; Uchiyama 2007). Ainu graves are usually oval or rectangular shaped. The dead were typically buried in an extended dorsal position, but some were buried in a crouched position (Hirakawa 1984). A variety of accessories were offered to the dead (Sekine 2003), but since different accessories were buried with men and women, it is often possible to guess the gender of the buried person even though no skeletal evidence remained. Furthermore, particular types of offerings are found around the head, which also makes it possible to estimate the head's orientation based on the distribution of burial accessories even though no skeletal remains were found (Utagawa 2007).

Utagawa Hiroshi has compiled and analyzed data from more than 1,000 burials belonging to the Pre-Modern Ainu and Modern Ainu Periods (Utagawa 2007). He noted that the burial orientation of the Pre-Modern Ainu (640 examples) was dominated by the eastern direction, as the data showed burial orientations of eastern (30.3 percent), southeastern (25.2 percent) and east-southeastern (17.5 percent) (Utagawa 2004b: 183). He also summarized the data, according to four major regions of four Ainu group: West Endiu (Yoichi Town), Sum-un-kur (Sapporo, Otaru, Ebetsu, Muroran Cities and Iburi, Oshima-Hiyama Regions), Sar-un-kur (Eniwa, Chitose, Tomakomai Cities; Biratori and Shin-Hidaka Town), and Menasi-un-kur (Mutsuishi, Erimo, Urakawa, Urahoro Towns; Kushiro-Nemuro and Okhotsk Sea Regions) (Table 7.1). This indicates that in the southwestern regions, Sum-un-kur and Sar-un-kur regions, east to southeastern orientation are dominant. In the West Endiu region, the northern orientation occupies a non-negligible ratio and in the Menas-un-kur region in eastern Hokkaido burials are often oriented from northeastern to north directions.

114 Cosmology in house and burial orientation

Table 7.1 Burial orientation by local Ainu group of the Pre-Modern Ainu period (based on Utagawa 2004b)

Groups/direction	N	NNE	ENE	E	ESE	SSE	S	Total
West Endiu (Yoichi City)	–	–	12	11	19	–	–	42
Sum-un-kur	–	–	–	152	63	56	–	271
Sar-un-kur	–	–	–	16	39	70	–	125
Menas-un-kur	51	12	18	20	15	–	–	116
Total	51	12	30	199	136	126	0	554

Since this data was mostly based on magnetic north, I have reanalyzed some 400 burials whose orientation has been numerically shown (Goto 2018). The offset of magnetic north from true north is approximately 9 degrees west on the basis of present Hokkaido data. I have hypothetically calibrated the orientation data by using this offset value for this histogram and other figures in this research.

At the Suehiro Burial of Chitose City (Figure 7.4: 3) in the Shikari-Chitose Region, 30 burials of the Pre-Modern Period have been excavated. Here, 80 percent of the burials are oriented from the northeast to the south-southeast zone and only three examples oriented toward north or west-northwest (Figure 7.8: a). The eastern to southeastern orientations are found in adjacent Karinba 2 (Figure 7.4: 1; Figure 7.8: b) and Usakumai (Figure 7.4: 4; Figure 7.8: c) sites in the Ishikari-Chitose Region. Note that all of these sites are located in the Sar-un-kur region.

There is some ethnographic evidence suggesting that exceptional burials were given for people who died in a somewhat abnormal manner (Ohtsuka 1964; Fujimoto 1971). By interviewing Ainu informants from Iburi Region, Yoshida Iwao noted that the dead should be buried by orienting their heads to east. If their heads were oriented to the west, they might become *oni* 鬼 (the Japanese term meaning "demon"). If the people were buried orienting their heads to the west, it was believed that the person would be reborn as a rabbit. Additionally, the person who met an unnatural death should be buried orienting their head to the east but slightly tilted to the north (Yoshida 1952: 304).

A similar eastern orientation of Pre-Ainu burials, with a few exceptions, are found in the southwestern regions, such as the Minamikawa Site (Figure 7.4: 5; Figure 7.8: d) in Tomari Town of the Oshima Peninsular, Ifirune (Figure 7.4: 6; Figure 7.8: e), and Ohkawa Ukai Point (Figure 7.4: 7; Figure 7.8: f) sites in Yoichi Town. Note that Tomari is in the Sum-un-kur region and the two sites in Yoichi are located in the West Endiu region that has a similarity with Southern Sakhalin Ainu (Kono 1931; Uchiyama 2006).

Cosmology in house and burial orientation 115

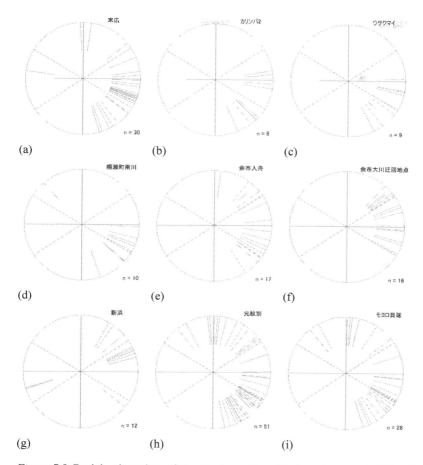

Figure 7.8 Burial orientation of Pre-Modern Ainu, Modern Ainu, and Okhotsk Periods.

Notes
a: Suehiro, b: Karinba, c: Usakumai, d: Minamikawa, e: Irifune (Yoichi), f: Ukai-chiten (Yoichi), g: Shinhama, h: Motomonbetsu, i: Moyoro.

I also show two recent burials of Shinhama in Erimo Town (circa 1900 to circa 1935) (Figure 7.4: 8; Figure 7.8: g), and the Moto-monbetsu burial (after 1868) (Figure 7.4: 9; Figure 7.8: h) in Montebtsu City. In contrast to modern burials (1904 to circa 1960) at Toyohata in Shi-Hidaka Town, Sar-un-kur region, where most burials were oriented to the southwest (Goto 2018), the Nihama site (Menas-un-kur region) burials tend to be oriented to the northeast. A northern orientation is more clearly indicated in the

116 *Cosmology in house and burial orientation*

Moto-monbetsu burials on the Okhotsk Sea coast, where there are also some cases of "abnormal" burials.

It is not conclusive whether regional variation in burial orientation came from temporal factors or regional ones. In the Satsumon Period, which preceded the Pre-Ainu Period, the burials with skeletal remains are not numerous, but Utagawa noted that the burial orientation tends to be from east to south (Utagawa 1992).

On the other hand, the influence of the Okhotsk culture that was contemporaneous with Satsumon culture could have contributed to regional variation of burials. For instance, at Moyoro Shell mound in Abashiri City on the Sea of Okhotsk (Figure 7.4: 10), 80 percent of burials have northwestern orientations (Figure 7.8: i) (Fujimoto 1965). One interpretation of this orientation is that it was the direction of the homeland of the Okhotsk people. In addition, burials of the Southern Sakhalin Ainu or Pre-Ainu periods tend to be oriented from north to west in Southern Sakhalin (Niioka and Utagawa 1990; Utagawa 2001: 58–461; Uchiyama 2006: 39–40).

The Ainu bear ceremony is considered to be inherited from the Okhotsk culture (e.g., Watanabe 1974; Amano 2003). Figure 7.9 shows the accumulation of bear skulls at the Okhotsk house site at the Moyori Shell mound. Therefore, one factor producing regional variation in burial orientation could be its inheritance from previous cultures.

Figure 7.9 Accumulation of bear skulls in the pit dwelling site at Moyoro Shell Mound Museum (an annex of Abashiri City Municipal Museum).

Discussion

There was significant regional variation in both house and burial orientations among the Hokkaido Ainu. In the southwestern region, eastward orientation was observed in both house and burial orientations, but the "east" had a broad meaning, *cup-ka*. In the north and eastern regions, dwelling structures and burial orientations were more variable and on the Okhotsk Sea coast, burials seem to be often directed toward from north to west.

Ainu cosmology was a complex system that consisted of river direction, the sacred mountain, the contrast between sea and mountains, as well as the sunrise and sunset directions. In addition, the regional variation of Ainu culture could have derived from previous cultures, such as the Satsumon culture and the Okhotsk culture.

The dominance of eastern orientation burials mainly found in southwestern areas accords with folklore that says that if the buried people with their heads being oriented to the east (face up) wake up, he/she would be facing the west, where the dead were supposed to go. This is so the dead would never get lost on their journey. Therefore, the west was more important to the dead than the east in the case of the eastern-oriented burials. Thus, eastern orientations of the sacred window and that of burials seem to have very different meanings.

In the Tokachi Region, there is an oral history saying that the sacred window was situated toward either west or north, but that recently this tradition was fading, and the window tends to be located on the eastern side (Yoshida 1952: 117). Considering this, I hypothesize that the houses without an entrance chamber and with the sacred window facing upriver or toward the sacred mountain were of the old type. Thereafter, a new ideological wave originated in southwestern Hokkaido, which distinguished the new type of houses with an entrance chamber and an eastern-oriented sacred window.

The Ainu of the southwestern region corresponds, to a large extent, with the group called Sar-un-kur, whose dialect and material culture (e.g., the decoration of *inaw*) were somewhat distinct from other groups. Kono Hiromichi, who analyzed the variation of burial poles, argued that "Sar-un-kur is a kind of island that had been wedged into other groups" (Kono 1931: 148). Ohyi further argued that the Ainu of southwestern Hokkaido (Sum-un-kur, including, Sar-un-kur, in his opinion) migrated from northern Honshu around the tenth century (Ohyi 1995). Both Kono and Ohyi provided oral and written evidence of such migration.

The group in the southwestern regions certainly had a longer contact period with the Japanese than eastern groups. Moreover, this region was relatively warm and the cultivation of millet was important. As a result, the population density was higher than in other regions (Kono 1931, 1932).

The emphasis on the sunrise direction of the southwestern group, which overlaps Sum-un-kur and Sar-un-kur, could be a custom that developed later. I argue that the comparison with Pueblo groups in North America, concerning the different emphasis of the sun (e.g., Hopi vs. Navajo), will be a promising topic to be explored in the future (e.g., Williamson 1987).

References

Ainu Bunka Hozon Taisaku Kyougikai [Ainu Culture Preservation Council] アイヌ文化保存対策協議会 (ed.)
    1969   *Ainu Ethnography, 2 Volumes.* 『アイヌ民族誌』2巻 Tokyo: Daiichihoki.
Amano, Tetsuya 天野哲也
    2003   *The Origin of Bear Ceremony.* 『クマ祭の起源』 Tokyo: Yuzankaku.
Batchelor, the Ven John
    1927   *Ainu Life and Lore: Echoes of a Departing Race.* Tokyo: Kyobunkwan.
Eniwa Shi Kyoiku Iinkai [Eniwa City Board of Education] 恵庭市教育委員会
    2005   *An Archaeologial Report on Point B at Karinba Site 1.* 『カリンバ1遺跡 B 地点調査 報告書』 Eniwa City.
Fujimoto, Hideo 藤本英夫
    1971   *Burials in the North.* 『北の墓』 Tokyo: Gakuseisha. (In Japanese).
Fujimoto, Tsuyoshi 藤本強
    1965   Burial of the Okhotsk Culture. 「オホーツク文化の葬制について」. *Busshitsu Bunka* 6: 15–30.
Fujimura, Hisakazu 藤村久和
    1985   *The Ainu Who Live with Gods.* 『アイヌ、神と生きる人々』 Tokyo: Fukutake Shoten.
Goto, Akira 後藤　明
    2018   House and burial orientations of the Hokkaido Ainu, indigenous hunter-gatherers of northern Japan. *Mediterranean Archaeology and Archaeometry* 18 (2): 173–180
Hayashi, Kensaku 林謙作
    1977   A preliminary consideration of the cosmology of the Ainu with specific reference to the monodirection Hypothesis. 「御殿山墳墓群ノ埋葬頭位ヲ論シ併セテあいぬ族ノ 他界観ニ及フ」 *Hoppo Bunka Kenkyu* 11: 1–28.
Hirakawa, Yoshinaga 平川善祥
    1984   An archaeological study of the Ainu burial in the Early-Modern Period. 「近世アイヌ 墳墓の考古学的研究」 In: Ishizuki, K. (ed.), *Study of Hokkaido: Archaeology II*, pp. 376–418. 『北海道の研究 2 』(考古学編 II) Osaka: Seibundo.
Hokkaido Bunka Hogo Kyokai [Hokaido Cultural Property Preservation Office] 北海道文化財保護協会

1989   *Urgent Field Research on Ethnograpy of the Ainu*, Vol 8 (Mukawa & Usu). 『アイヌ民俗文化財調査報告書』8巻：　鵡川　有珠地方 Hokkaido Board of Education, Hokkaido Governmental Office.

1990   *Urgent Field Research on Ethnograpy of the Ainu*, Vol 9 (Chitose). 『アイヌ民俗文化 財調査報告書』9 巻：　千歳 Hokkaido Board of Education, Hokkaido Government Office.

Hokkaido Kyoiku Iinkai [Hokkaido Board of Education] 北海道教育委員会

1986   *Urgent Field Research on Ethnograpy of the Ainu*, Vol 5 (Kushiro & Abashiri). 『アイヌ民俗文化財調査報告書』5巻：　釧路　網走地方 Hokkaido Government Office.

1987   *Urgent Field Research on Ethnograpy of the Ainu*, Vol 6 (Tokachi & Abashiri). 『アイヌ民俗文化財調査報告書』6巻：　十勝　網走地方 Hokkaido Governmental Office.

Kadosaski, Masaaki 門崎允昭

2016   *The Ainu and the Brown Bear: the Bear Ceremony*. 『アイヌ民族と羆』Sapporo: Hokkaido Shuppan Kikaku Center.

Kobayashi, Koji 小林孝二

2010   *Reconsideration on Architectural Culture of the Ainu*. 『アイヌの建築文化再考』Sapporo: Hokkaido Shuppan Kikaku Center.

Kono, Hiromichi 河野弘道

1931   A descent of an Ainu: Sarunkur. 「アイヌの一系統サルンクルに就て」*Jinruigak Zasshi* 47 (4): 137–148.

1932   Several descents of the Ainu seen from burial poles. 「墓標の型式より見たるアイヌの 諸系統」 *Ezoorai* 2 (4): 101–121.

Kubodera, Itsuhiko 久保寺逸彦

2001   *Religion and Ritual of the Ainu*. 『アイヌの宗教と儀礼』 Tokyo: Sofusha.

Matsui, Tomo 松井友

1999   *In the Bosom of the Fire God (Apefuchi-no-kamuy): Ainu Cosmology Told by an Old Lady*. 『火の神(アペフチカムイ)の懐にて―ある古老が語ったアイヌのコスモロジー 』 Tokyo:Yosensha.

Niioka, Takehiko and Hiroshi Utagawa 新岡武彦・宇田川洋

1990   *Archaeological Sites from Southern Sakhalin*. 『サハリン南部の遺跡』 Sapporo: Hokkaido Shuppan Kikaku Center.

Ohtsuka, Kazuyoshi 大塚和義

1964   Burial sites in Hokkaido. 「北海道の墓址」 *Busitsu Bunka* 4: 3–58.

Ohyi, Haruo 大井晴夫

1995   A reconsideration on the Battle of *Shaku-shain* (1669). 「シャクシャインの乱(寛文9年　蝦夷の乱)」の再検討」 *Hoppo Bunka Kenkyu* 22: 1–116.

Sekine, Tatsuto 関根達人

2003   Offerings in the Ainu burials. 「アイヌ墓の副葬品」 *Bussitsu Bunka* 376–418.6: 38–54.

Sueoka, Tomio 末岡外美男

1979   *Stars of the Ainu*. 『アイヌの星』 Asahikawa Municipal Library.

2009 *Stars and Legends of the Ainu-tari.* 『人間達[アイヌタリ]のみた星座と伝承』 Asahikawa: Private Publishing.

Uchida, Yuichi
   1998 Regional variation of *cise*: based on Tokachi Ainu. In: The Ainu Museum (ed.), *Considering Ainu's Residence, chine, Shiraoi*, pp. 112–126. Shiraoi: The Ainu Museum.

Uchiyama, Tatsuya 内山達也
   2005 The concept of afterlife of the Ainu. 「アイヌの他界観」 *Bussitsu Bunka Kenkyu* 2: 1–26.
   2006 A consideration of burial custom of Sakhalin Ainu. 「樺太アイヌの埋葬形態についての 一考察」 *Busshitsu Bunka Kenkyu*, 3: 32–51.
   2007 Ainu orientation system: an essay of the direction of sacred window and burial orientation based on the examples from Biratori Town). 「アイヌの方位観 : 神窓方位と埋葬頭位に 関する一試論（平取を中心として）」 *Busshitsu Bunka Kenkyu* 4: 11–36.

Utagawa, Hiroshi 宇田川洋
   1992 The formation process of Ainu burials: an aspect of the Ainu Culture seen from archaeology. 「アイヌの墓の成立過程 : 考古学からみたアイヌ文化の一側面」 In: Okada, H. and A. Okada (eds.), *Anthropology in the North.* 岡田宏明 岡田厚子編 『北の人類学』, pp. 237–281. Kyoto: Akademia Shuppan.
   2001 *The Study of Ainu Archaeology: Introduction.* 『アイヌ考古学序説』 Sapporo: Hokkaido Shuppan Kikaku Center.
   2004a *The Iomante of Bears and Awls.* 『クマとフクロウのイオマンテ』 Tokyo: Doseisha.
   2004b Chashi sites and Ainu burials. In: Nomua T. and H. Utagawa (eds.), *Satsumon and Ainu Culture* 「チャシ跡とアイヌ墓」 野村崇 宇田川洋編 『擦文 アイヌ文化』, pp. 170–193. Sapporo: Hokkaido Shinbunsha.
   2007 *Figures of Ainu Burial of Remains Grave Collection.* 『アイヌ葬送墓集成図』 SapporoHokkaido Shuppan Kikaku Center.

Watanabe, Hitoshi
   1974 The origin of the Ainu Culture: particularly in relation to the Okhotsk Culture. *Kokogaku Zasshi* 58 (3): 47–64.
   1990 Worship of Sacred mountains among northern hunter-gatherers: a functional interpretation based on the Ainu case. 「北方狩猟民の聖山信仰 : アイヌを中心とする機能的概観」 In: Y. Kotani (ed.), *Comparative Studies of Northern Cultures* 『北方諸文化の比較研究』, pp. 237–279. Nagoya: Nagoya University.

Williamson, Ray A.
   1987 *Living the Sky: The Cosmos of the American Indian.* Norman: University of Oklahoma Press.

Yoshida, Iwao 吉田巌
   1952 Memories of Kosankean Furukawa: Ainu ethnography as told by an Old Tokachi Ainu. 「古川コサンケアン翁談叢」 *Minzokugaku Kenkyu*, 16 (3,4): 300–310.

8 The sun and the Kingdom of Ryukyu
An ethnohistorical approach to state formation

Archaeological background

The earliest human occupation of the Ryukyu Islands is traced back to 35,000 BCE and the oldest human remains that have been found in Japan have come from these islands (Kaifu et al. 2015). The Shell Mound Period began around 5000 BCE, which was based on a foraging economy and developed a distinctive pottery style. From the tenth to twelfth centuries, foraging had shifted to an agricultural economy and this marked the beginning of the Gusuku Period (circa eleventh century CE). *Gusuku* literally means "castle" (城) and many fortifications were constructed throughout the islands. *Gusuku* were residences for local chiefs and their followers and included a sacred shrine. In this period, social stratification was marked by agriculture and livestock domestication (Asato 1990).

On Okinawa's Main Island, the Ryukyu Kingdom united local powers at the end of the Gusuku Period and flourished between the fifteenth and nineteenth centuries. The Kingdom also extended its trade relations with China and Southeast Asia (Irumada and Tomiyama 2002).

The gusuku period

Several possibilities exist about the origin of *gusuku*. There is enormous variation in their shape and structure, but we find one fixed pattern in *gusuku* sites: there is always a sacred place or alter within the *gusuku* and this sacred place is still worshiped today. Probably the place that was originally worshiped as a sacred place was used for practical purposes, such as providing lodging for chiefs or for fortification (Nakamatsu 1992).

Local chiefs in the thirteenth to fourteenth centuries competed with each other by trading with China and Southeast Asia to obtain prestigious goods, such as ceramics and iron tools, and distributed them to their followers. Small chiefdoms were united into three kingdoms in the early

122 *The sun and the Kingdom of Ryukyu*

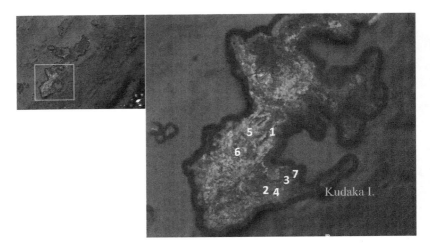

Figure 8.1 Okinawa Main Island and archaeological sites and monuments mentioned in this chapter.

Notes
1: Naka Gusuku, 2: Itokazu Gusuku, 3: Chinen Gusuku, 4: Tama Gusuku, 5: Urasoe Gusku, 6: Shuri Castle, 7: Seifa Utaki.

fourteenth century: the Northern Kingdom 北山(山北), the Central Kingdom 中山, and the Southern Kingdom 南山(山南). The three kingdoms were finally united by the Central Kingdom and this marked the beginning of the Ryukyu Kingdom.

The Ryukyu Kingdom consists of two dynasties: the First Sho 尚 Dynasty (1406–1468), and the Second Sho Dynasty (1470–1879). The *Omoro-soshi* is a collection of chants compiled between 1531 and 1632 by the Second Sho Dynasty and is full of terms that portray the king as the sun.

During the era of the King Shonei 尚寧, the Satsuma Clan, the southernmost clan of Kyushu Island, had invaded the Ryukyu Kingdom in 1609. At this time, the Satsuma Clan subordinated the Ryukyu Kingdom but allowed it to operate independently since the Satsuma Clan wanted to take advantage of the imported goods from China and Southeast Asia that the Ryukyu Kingdom had obtained through trade. Through this trade, Chinese geomancy and calendar system were introduced. Also, throughout the islands, there were marine stations that oversaw the arrival and departure of ships.

In 1879, the Ryukyu Kingdom came to an end after the Tokugawa government collapsed due to civil war. The Ryukyu Islands today are called Okinawa Prefecture (Asato 1990, 1998; Irumada and Tomiyama 2002).

Gates of *gusuku* castles

The *Omoro-soshi* contains several chants explaining how the gates of *gusuku* were to be constructed toward the east. One example of this is the chant referred to as Naka Gusuku (Figure 8.1: 1), which is also the name of one of the great castles constructed in the fifteenth century.

kikoe naka-gusuku/agaruini mukate/itiyadija tatenaotihe
(famous naka-gusuku)/(east, directed to)/(plank-gate, re-built)

Translation: "In the famous Naka Gusuku castle, a plank gate was re-built toward the east."

toyomu naka-gusuku/tedaga-anani mukaite
(famous naka-gusuku)/(hole of the sun, directed to)
(Song 42 in Volume 2: Hokama 2000)

Translation: "In the renown Naka Gusuku castle, a gate was rebuilt toward the hole of the sun."

Here, the expression "*aragui-ni-mukete*" is translated as "directing toward the east." "*Agaruï*" literally means "rising (of the sun)" and is thus translated as "east." But this does not mean true east. That the gate that was "rebuilt" seems to suggest the gate opened at the wall of the additional square of the castle or a newly built section, and this gate opens to the direction of east-northeast, probably corresponding to June solstice of this location (Figure 8.2: a and b). In this case, "*agaruï*" seems to refer to the direction of June solstice. In the indigenous orientation system of the Ryukyu Islands, there is a possibility that "north" means north-northeast (the direction of *ushi*, cow) and "east" means east-northeast (the direction of *tatsu*, dragon) (Kojima 1987; Tarama Sonshi Henshu Iinkai 1993: 339).

The same is true of Itokazu Gusuku 糸数城 (Figure 8.1: 2), Chinen Gusuku 知念城 (Figure 8.1: 3), and Tama Gusuku 玉城城 (Figure 8.1: 4). The gates of these castles were directed toward east-northeast, although present vegetation hinders the view of the eastern sky. A special mention should be made about Tama Gusuku (Figure 8.3), which is constructed on a hill. The *gusuku* gate was usually constructed by piling square rocks, but the gate of Tama Gusuku was made by drilling a hole in a huge rock (Figure 8.3: a and b). It must have been easier to make a gate by piling rocks, but builders intentionally formed a hole into the rock toward the June solstice.

In this spot, I have observed that the June solstice sun rises through the gate (Figure 8.3: c), and sunlight radiates onto the most sacred altar in the

124 *The sun and the Kingdom of Ryukyu*

(a)
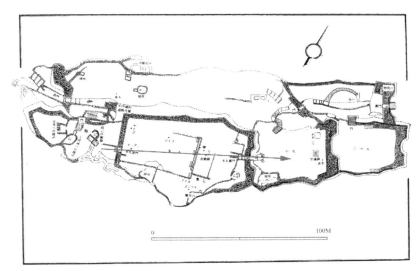

(b)

Figure 8.2 Naka Gusuku Castle.

Notes
a The plan of the castle (arrow indicates the direction of Naka-mon gate; modified from Okinawaken Kyoiku Iinkai Bunkaka ed. 1983: Figure 26).
b Naka-mon gate.

The sun and the Kingdom of Ryukyu 125

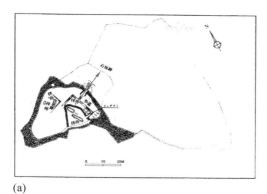
(a)

(b)

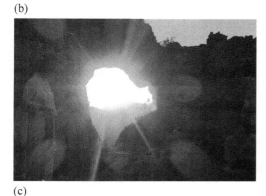
(c)

Figure 8.3 Tamagusuku Castle.

Notes
a Plan of Tamagusuku Castle (arrow indicates the direction of main gate; modified from Okinawaken Kyoiku Iinkai Bunkaka 1983, Figure 45).
b The gate of Tamagusuku Castle.
c June solstice sun rise through the gate.

castle. I argue that this artificial hole is related to the belief of *teda-ga-ana* (the hole of the sun), which refers to the hole of the sun in the eastern sea. In the *Omoro-sohi*, we often find such expressions as:

> *agarui kogane ana/agarui no mashita-ni/teda-ga-ana no mashita-ni*
> (east, golden hole)/(east, right under)/(hole of the sun, right under)
> (Hokama 2000: Vol 4)

A series of chants singing that the gate was directed toward the east does not mean that the gate opened toward true east, but rather the gate probably opened toward June solstice. There are many chants that proclaim that the priestess introduced sunlight to the sacred place of the castle. I interpret these chants as follows: *noro*, the official priestess, introduced *sezi* (sacred power, a similar concept to that of Polynesian *mana*), symbolized by sunlight, into the sacred place, *ibi*, for the fertility of the kingdom (Ikemiya 1990; Suetsugu 1995).

Archaeologist Susumu Asato found that the alignment of the palaces of local chiefs before and after the unification tends to shift from south or east to west. He interpreted this as suggesting that the palaces facing the south or east were constructed before the unification and reflected the idea of introducing *sezi*, sacred power from the sun. On the other hand, after the unification, the royal palace at Shuri Castle was built facing westward and reflects the idea of the king himself being the sun (or a child of the sun), radiating sunlight toward the people (Asato 2006).

Three kingdom period and the unification of the islands

According to the *Chuzan Seifu* 『中山世譜』 and *Chuzan Seikan* 『中山世鑑』, royal histories of the islands, the Ryukyu Kingdom was founded by the chiefly clans of Urasoe Castle 浦添城 in the fifteenth century (Figure 8.4: a). Urasoe is located 5 km north of Shuri, where the Ryukyu Dynasty ultimately settled (Figure 8.1: 5). Before coming to Shuri, there were ten generations in the Urasoe chiefly lineage whose genealogical history was not linear at all. The chiefly genealogy actually consists of three discontinuous lineages.

The first king Shunten 舜天 is said to have been a son of Minamoto Tametomo 源為朝, a legendary samurai hero. Legend has it that after being defeated by rival samurai clans in Kyoto, Tametomo was banished to Izu Islands, south of Tokyo, but he escaped by boat and instead traveled to the Ryukyu Islands. This legend is found throughout the Ryukyu Islands but does not seem to have actually occurred. The legend continues to say that thereafter Shunten was born to him and became the first king of the

The sun and the Kingdom of Ryukyu 127

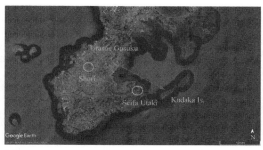
(a)

(b)

(c)

Figure 8.4 Urasoe Castle and Kudaka Island.

Notes
a Direction of Kudaka Island seen from Urasoe Castle.
b Kudaka Island seen from Hanareji rock.
c Winter solstice sun rise behind Kudaka Island, seen from Urasoe Castle.

Urasoe Dynasty, although there is a controversy of the real existence of early kings of said dynasty (Yoshinari 2018). Shunten's lineage continued for three generations, but Eiso who was not the direct descent of Shunten became the fourth king by abdication of an emperor in favor of a more virtuous successor: *"zenjo"* (禅譲), which is the Chinese philosophy of ideal succession of the emperorship.

Regarding the legend that Shunten was the son of Tametomo, on the southeastern end of the Urasoe Castle there is a rock called Tametomo Rock or *Hanareji* 離れ岩, meaning "separated rock" in the Ryukyu dialect (Figure 8.4: b). Looking toward the southeast from this rock, the sun of the December solstice is seen to rise above the middle of Kudaka Island, which is the most sacred island in the kingdom (Figure 8.4: c). In the *Omoro-soshi* chants, there is a frequently used expression, *teda-ga-ana*, which means "the hole of the sun." Since Kudaka Island is a low island, if seen from Urasoe Castle, the sun appears to rise from the hole of the sun at the horizon (Kojima 1987).

Further, there is a royal tomb in Urasoe Castle called Urosoe Youdore. This tomb is said to have been constructed by the fourth king of Urasoe Dynasty, King Eiso 英祖 (1260–1299). This belief came from a description found in the *Chuzan Seikan* and *Kyuyo* 『球陽』. Here, I refer to the opinion that the foundation of this tomb is later, probably in the fourteenth century. According to this opinion, the founder of this tomb could not be Eiso (Yoshinari 2018).

King Eiso is often described as the child of the sun and he is considered the key person in the development of solar ideology within the dynasty. Legend has it that the wife of Chief Iso had a dream of the sun coming into her breast and she became pregnant the next morning. The child she gave birth to is said to be King Eiso. When grown, he became the king by *"zenjo"* succession. Later kings of the Sho Dynasty often referred to King Eiso to ascertain their royal status of the solar dynasty (Asato 2006: 60–61).

The tomb consists of two spaces surrounded by stone walls under the high cliff. Going down to the tomb from the castle, we see Kudaka Island on the descent. When going through the first gate, Kurashinujo 暗しん御門 (dark gate), one comes into the dark front yard. Before being destroyed during World War II, this yard functioned as a tunnel. If we go further through the second gate, Nakaujo Gate 中御門 (middle gate) (Figure 8.5: a), we suddenly come to the bright main yard surrounded by white shining coral rocks (Figure 8.5: b). Here lie royal tombs including the grave of King Eiso. According to Asato, the approach from the dark front yard to the bright main yard may symbolize the shift from the dark world of death to the heavenly world, *nirai-kanai*, full of sunlight (Asato 2006: 53–60).

The sun and the Kingdom of Ryukyu 129

(a)

(b)

Figure 8.5 Urasoe Youdore a: Nakaujo gate, b: Main graveyard.
Notes
a: Nakaujo gate; b: Main graveyard.

Interestingly, the sun of December solstice is seen to rise just over the Nakamon Gate that connects the world of darkness and that of light. Seen from this tomb, the direction to Kudaka Island appears to be the direction of the heavenly world.

The last King of the Urasoe Dynasty, King Satto 察度, who lived in the latter half of the fourteenth century, was invited to Shuri Castle to construct a new capital, again by *"zenjo"* succession. King Satto was succeeded by his son Bunei 武寧, but King Bunei was later defeated by the Sho Clan. The Sho Clan then founded the Sho Dynasty at the beginning of the fifteenth century and they defeated Northern and Southern Kingdoms, which united the islands. The First Sho Dynasty continued for seven generations and the Second Sho Dynasty continued for 19 generations (Asato 2006).

The sacred Kudaka Island

Kudaka Island 久高島 was the most sacred island in the Ryukyu Islands. The size of this island is only 1.38 km^2 and its maximum height is 17.5 m (Figure 8.6). This small island is known for the *Izaiho* ritual, which has been held every 12 years in the year of the horse. This ritual was last performed in 1978 and ceased thereafter. A series of rituals were held for five days until one day before the December solstice to initiate the priestess.

The inhabitants of the island consider the direction of sunrise to be sacred since there is an ideal space, *nira-hara* or *nirai-kanai*, from which gods visit the island. This place is also where ancestors live and where the fertility of crops and seafood came from. As already mentioned, the sun rises at *teda-ga-ana*, which lies toward the direction of *nirai-kanai*. The islanders pray toward this direction (eastward). On the other hand, the sun sets in the direction of *tida-banta*, which means "cliff where the sun hides" (Higa 1993).

The islanders consider the direction of the sunset to be impure. Once a year, they put harmful insects on a model raft made from banana trees and ritually drift them to this direction in order to prevent a crop failure due to an insect plague. On the island, there is a proverb saying that you should finish your wish before the sun crosses the meridian. The islanders consider that the sun is stronger before noon and is weaker afterward. The sacrifice to the dead and the ritual to remove harmful insects should be done in the afternoon. They also sacrifice the dead in this direction and the soul of the dead is considered to follow the setting sun. Both the sun and the souls go around the underground or under the sea and finally reach the *nira-hara* in the eastern sea (Wakugami 1992).

Kaberu Hama Beach is located at the northeastern corner of the island. Kaberu means "the field of gods" and this is the place where the heavenly

The sun and the Kingdom of Ryukyu 131

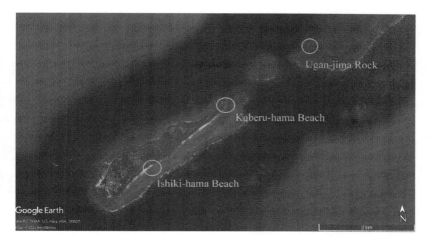

Figure 8.6 Kudaka Island.

god Amamikyo first ascended. On this beach, rituals are held in February and June of the lunar calendar. The summer ritual held on June solstice sunrise is *miruku-gwati*, meaning beautiful or new June when the sun is to be reborn. On this day, the sun god descends on the small rock in the sea and then it lands on this beach (Higa 1993). The rock is referred to as Ugan-jima, meaning "the island for prayer." The villagers said that the June solstice sun is seen to rise behind this rock. The trail is extended from this beach southwestward to the village and this trail is said to be the road of the sun. I suspect that this ritual is to introduce the strongest power of the sun on June solstice to the village.

Unlike many other islands, rice does not grow on this island. In contrast, the creation myth describes this island as the origin of wheat. Legend has it that a white shinning pot was drifting and beached on Ishiki Hama Beach 伊敷浜 on the east side of the island. When locals opened the pot, it contained seeds of five crops, one of which was wheat. The wheat was dedicated to the royal palace and the king thereafter visited this island to celebrate this event (Suetsugu 1995: 117–118).

There is another legend regarding the origin of wheat:

> The daughter of the founder of Kudaka Island served as a priestess in the royal palace. She was beautiful and loved by the king. She became his wife and became pregnant, but other women who were jealous harassed her said that the lady broke wind (farted). Being ashamed,

she returned to the island and begat a boy. The boy, when turning seven years old, went to Ishiki Hama Beach and prayed to the gods. After seven days, a golden gourd drifted to him. He dared to see the King Tamagusuku 玉城, the 4th king in royal lineage founded by "solar king" Eiso of (the 4th king of Urasoe chiefly lineage originated in Shunten) and dedicated the golden gourd to the king. He said to the king, "if a woman who never breaks wind plants it, it will produce a lot of fruits." The king realized his fault and came to know that this wise boy was his son. The king adopted him as his successor and the boy became the fifth King Seii 西威. After that, kings came to visit Kudaka Island to get the first crops of wheat and worshiped the sun at this beach.

(Suetsugu 1995: 117–118)

The legend of a shining pot or golden gourd drifting to the Ishik Hama Beach, the place to pray for the sun, indicates the origin of wheat was closely related to sun worship.

Solar kingdom in Shuri

After the unification of the islands by the Sho Dynasty in the Shuri district of Naha City, there was a growing tendency to see the king as the sun itself. The *Omoro-soshi* is full of such expressions. For example:

shuri owaru, tedakoka/tama, isigaki, kerahete
(in Shuri, live, child of the sun)/(beautiful, stonewall, built)

Translation: "In Shuri Castle lives a child of the sun (i.e., the king), he built a beautiful stonewall" [No. 217 song in Volume 5: Hokama 2000].

These expressions clearly indicate that the worship of the sun occupies the central role in the ritual of the kingdom.

As already mentioned, *teda* means "the sun" and *teda-ko* means "the child of the sun." *Teda* is a symbolic expression applied to kings as well as to local chiefs, but *teda-ko* is used only for the king. There is a possibility that *teda* was originally a symbolic expression to someone with political power, such as *aji* 按司 (local chiefs), but *teda-ko*, child of the sun, was specifically used to symbolize king or paramount chief (Fuku 2002). There is another possibility that the expression *teda-ko* was created during the Shuri Dynasty, or at the era of King Shoshin 尚真 of Second Sho Dynasty, in particular, and that *teda* was given to local chiefs in order to legitimate the subordination of local chiefs to Shuyi Dynasty (Suetsugu 1995: 166–167; Yoshinari 2018: 226–233).

The sun and the Kingdom of Ryukyu 133

In the Ryukyu Dynasty, there is a historical record that notes that locals performed the new year ritual on December solstice and the New Year (Irumada and Tomiyama 2002: 229). During this ritual, the king stood at the balcony of the palace and faced westward (Asato 2006: 46–47). The followers in the royal garden looked up eastward at the king symbolizing himself as a sun god. This ritual was clearly of Chinese influence, since in China, at the December solstice ritual, the king worshiped the north direction (i.e., Polaris and the Forbidden City of Beijing 紫禁城) (Ikemiya 1990).

At Shuri Royal Castle, when a king died his corpse was carried out from the Kankaimon Gate 歓会門, which is located in the northwest of the palace. On the other hand, when the new king came up to the palace for the first time, he passed through two particular gates, the Keiseimon Gate (継世門), meaning "the gate for succession (of the King)," and the Bifukumon Gate (美福門), meaning "beautiful and happy gate." These gates, which are located at the southeast of the palace, were usually used only by women officials, but at the time of succession, they were used by the new king. He passed from the eastern end of the castle through Keiseimon and Bifukumon and moved westward to the palace (Figure 8.7: a). Thus, the

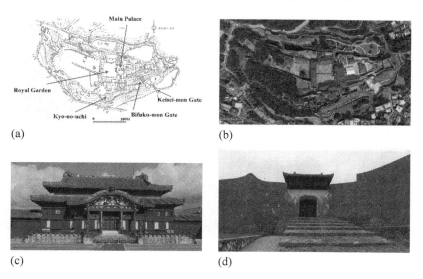

Figure 8.7 Shuri Castle.

Notes
a Plan of Shuri Castle (modified from Okinawaken Kyoiku Iinkai Bunkaka 1975: 32).
b Shuri Castle seen from Google Earth.
c Reconstructed Main Palace facing west (burnt down in October 2019).
d Keisei-mon Gate.

new king behaved as would a rising sun. Also, when the king died, the coffin of the king was carried out through the gate located on the west side of the castle (Maehira 1989; Suetsugu 1995: 183) (Figure 8.7: b). The main palace is facing the west. Therefore, if the king stood at the balcony, he must have been facing the followers sitting below as the sun.

Dual kingship

After the unification of the kingdom, the ritual of receiving sunlight continued and it was held by official priestesses. In the Ryukyu Islands, there is a belief that women are more sacred than men. This belief is called *onarigami* and suggests that men are guarded by their close relatives, such as aunts or sisters.

Through the process of establishing the Shuri Dynasty, a gender division of the roles developed: kings were seen as a sun to govern the kingdom and the women were seen as priestesses to take on a religious role. This is a type of dual kingship that consists of combining the male political authority and female sacred power. *Kikoe-ookimi* (聞得大君) is the highest priestess and she was *onarigami* to the king (Nakamatsu 1992).

In the *Omoro-soshi*, there are many chants that associate the king with the sun:

> *shuri no teda to/tenn ni teru tedato/madijyuni chiyoware*
> (Shuri, in, sun and)/(in the heaven, shinning sun, too/(be united, as a whole)

Translation: "The sun in Shuri (the king) and the sun in heaven should be united together" [Song 212, in Vol. 5: Hokama 2000].

In Shuri Castle, there is a sacred space called *kyo-no-uchi* (京之内) (Figure 8.8: a), where only priestesses could enter and there they would worship the sun to introduce the sacred power to the King's palace and everywhere else in the country. At certain times of the year, the priestesses opened the sacred doors to introduce sunlight into this space. Concerning this custom, there is an *Omoro-soshi* chant that states: "Let *kikoe-ookimi* (the highest priestess) and king work in close cooperation to protect this country where the sun is shining beautifully." The symbolism that depicted the king as the sun and *kikoe-ookimi* working in cooperation may symbolize the motif of "primordial pair and sacred marriage (*Hieros gamos*)" seen in the creation myth of the Ryukyu Islands.

There are different opinions about whether Kudaka Island was visible from Shuri Castle or not. However, the Sho Dynasty founded the Benga Mine Utaki Shrine on the eastern side of the castle to worship Kudaka

Island and constructed a stone-paved road for easy access by the priestess and the king to this shrine (Suetsugu 2012). In *Ryukyukoku Yuraiki* (*The Origin of the Ryukyu Kingdom*) 『琉球国由来記』, Vol. 1, there is a description that the king worshiped Kudaka Island from the Benga Mine Utaki Shrine. In the small shrine on this sacred place, we could see an epitaph of important kings of both the Urasoe and Sho Dynasty, such as Shunten, Eiso, Satto and so on, suggesting continuous worship of Kudaka Island for sun ritual from Urasoe to Shuri Dynasties.

Lastly, Seifa-Utaki shrine is the most sacred shrine since the succession rite of *kikoe-ookimi* was held here. Seifa-Utaki is located on the southeastern coast of Okinawa Island, facing Kudaka Island (Figure 8.8: a). In particular, the sacred space behind the divided rocks was also the place to worship Kudaka Island. The white sand collected from Kudaka Island was spread on the ground to purify the shrine.

At the succession ritual, *kikoe-ookimi* was supposed to arrive at this shrine in the evening. After praying at the three altars at midnight, she was then supposed to sleep in a temporary palace in front of the shrine. In her

(a)

(b)

Figure 8.8 Seifa-Utaki.

Notes
a Sacred rocks.
b Kudaka Island seen from the inside of sacred rocks.

bed, two golden pillows were prepared: one pillow for *kikoe-ookimi* and another pillow for the god, probably the sun god coming from Kudaka Island. They say that when the first sunlight coming from behind the Kudaka Island shines (Figure 8.8: b). This is again a motif symbolizing a sacred marriage.

Discussion

Solar kingship that sees the king as a child of the sun does not seem to have originated in the Ryukyu Islands. In the creation myth, the heavenly goddess Amamiku (or Amamikyo) descended to the earth or drifted to the island. The goddess created the islands and then settled the primordial seven shrines. Then Amamiku distributed the seed of crops such as rice on Tamagusuku, as well as wheat, millet, and others on Kudaka Island. Thus, in the creation myth, it seems the sun did not play a particularly important role.

In a previous chapter, I have pointed out that a rich star lore existed among the Ryukyu Islanders. In particular, they observed the rise of the Pleiades in the eastern sky at dusk as an index to wheat seeds. Additionally, indigenous beliefs believe it is natural to see the east as the sacred direction for praying for fertility. The aim to obtain sacred power from the sun was a widespread custom among villagers as well as chiefly clans. I pointed out that the gates of some castle sites had been reconstructed to be directed toward June solstice sunrise for the maximum effect of sunlight. The mention of either sunrise or sunset on June solstice is rare in the Shuri Dynasty Period, but there is one description in the *Ryukyukoku Yuraiki* that on a lucky day around June 1 in the lunar calendar, the gates of the Shuri Castle were opened in the early morning to introduce fortune. I suspect that this ritual is a remnant of "to open the gate toward eastward" (Nahashishi Hensan Iinkai 1968).

In historic records and the *Omoro-soshi* chants, the king was often described as a child of the sun and as a god, as evidenced by chants such as: "The sun in Shuri (the king) and the sun in heaven should be united together." (Hokama 2000). It seems that the king as the sun took a position as a heavenly god in the creation myth. In the Shuri Dynasty, the King himself became the sun, radiating for others by sacred power and the priestesses were continually supplying sacred power to the king. However, once a year, the king himself should be rejuvenated at a December solstice ritual that was inherited from the Urasoe Dynasty. It seems that the continual rebirth of the king as the child of the sun had become the central theme of the royal ritual of the Ryukyu Kingdom (Goto 2016).

After the unification of the islands by the Central Kingdom, there seems to have been a transformation of religious thought that was based on restructuring local beliefs about the sun to be integrated with the royal cosmology of the Ryukyu Kingdom. In this process, the worship of December solstice and Kudaka Island inherited from Urasoe Dynasty were transformed into elaborate royal rituals based on the dual structure of man/women: politics/religion. This resulted in the formation of the cosmovision that is significantly different from those of other parts of Japan.

References

Asato, Susumu 安里進
 1990 *History of Ryukyu Seen from Archaeology, Vol. 1.* 『考古学からみた琉球史、（上）』. Naha: Hirugisha.
 1998 *Gusuku, Community and Village: an Introduction to Okinawan Historical Archaeology.* 『グスク 共同体 村： 沖縄歴史考古学序説』 Ginowan: Yojyu-shobou.
 2006 *Kingship and Gusuku of Ryukyu.* 『琉球王権とグスク』 Tokyo: Yamakawa-shuppan.

Fuku, Hiromi 福寛美
 2002 The Sun God of Okinawa. 「沖縄の太陽神」 In: K. Matsumura and K. Watanabe (eds.), *A Study of the Sun God* 松村一雄 渡辺和子（編）『太陽神の研究』], pp. 171–190. Tokyo: Lithon.

Goto Akira
 2016 Solar Kingdom of Ryukyu: the formation of a cosmovision in the southern Islands of the Japanese Archipelago. *Journal of Astronomy in Culture* 1 (1): 173–180.

Higa, Yasuo 比嘉康雄
 1993 *Kudaka Island as a Homeland of Gods, 2 Vols.* 『神々の源境 久高島 2巻』 Tokyo: Daiichi-shobo.

Hokama, Shuzen 外間守善
 2000 *Omoro-soshi, Vol. 1.* 『おもろさうし、（上）』 Tokyo: Iwanami Shoten.

Ikemiya, Masaharu 池宮正治
 1990 Kingship ideology seen in *Omoro-soshi*. 「『おもろさうし』にみる王権思想」. *Shin-Okinawa-Bungaku* 85: 63–69.

Irumada Nori o 入間田宣男 and Kazuyuki Tomiyama 豊見山和行
 2002 *Hiraizumi in the North, and Ryukyu in the South.* 『北の平泉、 南の琉球』 Tokyo: Chuokoron.

Kaifu, Y., M. Fujita, M. Yoneda, S. Yamzaki
 2015 Pleistocene Seafaring and colonization of the Ryukyu Islands, southwestern Japan. In: Y. Kaifu, M. Izuho, M., T. Goebel, H. Sato, and A. Ono (eds.), *Emergence and Diversity of Modern Human Behavior in Paleolithic Asia*. College Station: Texas A & Am University Press.

Kojima Yoshiyuki 小島瓔禮
    1987   Shurijo Castle: Gods praising kingship. 「首里城： 王権を讃える神々」 In: K. Tanigawa (ed.), *Gods of Japan, Shrines and Sacred Places, Vol 13: Southwestern Islands* 谷川 健一編）『日本の 神々、神社と聖地、第13巻： 南西諸島』, pp. 133–167. Tokyo: Hakusui-sha.

Maehira, Bokei 真栄平房敬
    1989   *Story of Shurijo Castle*. 『首里城物語』 Naha: Hirugisha.

Nahashishi Hensan Iinkai [Naha City History Editorial Board] 那覇市史編纂委員会
    1968   *History of Naha City: Source Book, Vol. 1(1)*. 『那覇市史：資料編1巻(1)』、 Naha City Hall.

Nakamatsu, Yashu 仲松弥秀
    1992   Belief and sacred songs of Southern Islands. 「南島の信仰と神謡」 In: K. Tanigawa, (ed.), *The Sea and Culture of the Japanese Archipelago, Vol. 6: The World of Ryukyu Archipelago* 谷川健一（編）『海と列島文化 第6巻： 琉球弧の世界』, pp. 299–326. Tokyo: Shogakukan.

Okinawaken Kyoiku Iinkai Bunkaka [Cultural Division of Okinawa Prefectural Education Board] 沖縄県教育委員会文化課（編）
    1975   *A Report of Reconstruction of Kankaimon Gate, Shuri Castle*. 『首里城歓会門復元工事 報告書』、 Cultural Division of Okinawa Prefectural Education Board.
    1983   *A Report on the Distribution Okinawan Gusuku: Okinawa Island and Neighbour Islands*. 『沖縄グスク分布調査報告書： 沖縄本島及び周辺離島』. Ginowan: Ryokurindo.

Suetsugu, Satoshi 末次智
    1995   *Kingship and Myths of Ryukyu: A Study of Omoro-soshi*. 『琉球の王権と神話： 『おもろさうし』の研究』 Tokyo: Daiichi Shobou.
    2012   *A Consideration of Royal Songs: from Space and Time of Shuri Castle*. 『宮廷歌謡論： 首里城の時空から』 Tokyo: Shinwa-sha.

Tarama Sonshi Henshu Iinkai [Tayama Village History Editorial Board] 多良間村史編集委員会
    1993   *History of Tarama Village*. 『多良間村史』, Vol. 4 (3), Tarama Village Hall.

Wakugami, Motoo 湧上元雄
    1992   Kudaka Island and sacred religious service. In: K. Tanigawa (ed.), *The Sea and Culture of the Japanese Archipelago, Vol. 6: The World of Ryukyu Archipelago* 「久高島と神事」谷川健一（編）『海と列島文化 第6巻： 琉球弧の世界』, pp. 363–397. Tokyo: Shogakukan.

Yoshinari, Naoki 吉成直樹
    2018   *Kingship and King of the Sun in Ryukyu*. 『琉球王権と太陽の王』 Tokyo: Shichigatsusha.

9 Epilogue

An ethnologist, Oka Masao pointed out that Japanese culture is characterized by the coexistence of apparently contradictory features, such as conservatism vs. entrepreneurship. He argued that this results from the unique position of the Japanese Archipelago, which has been influenced by cultures from different parts of eastern Eurasia and southeast Asian islands. The Japanese have not only accepted these influences but also developed a mixed and multilayered cultural tradition without substantial political change stimulated from the outside for thousands of years (Oka 1979).

The nature of such elements of Japanese culture is observed in the cultural astronomy of the Japanese Archipelago. I believe that I could demonstrate some aspects of cultural diversity and traditionalism existing in Japan's cultural astronomy in this book. Cultural astronomy in the archipelago is both diverse and traditional in terms of the syncretism of animism, Shinto, Buddhism, Confucianism, and other elements (Chapters 1, 2, and 6). Further, the traditions of the Hokkaido Ainu and Ryukyu Islanders add further variation to this richness of cultural astronomy in the archipelago (Chapters 3 and 4).

In this book, I have examined issues of archaeoastronomy in terms of solar phenomena, such as the alignment of stone circles and burials of the Jomon Period (Chapter 5), house structure and burial orientation of the Pre-Modern Ainu (Chapter 7), and the alignment of *gusuku* in the Ryukyu Island (Chapters 8). Recently, however, other ways of interpreting these phenomena have been proposed. For instance, some argue that solar ideology in the Ryukyu Kingdom developed in a later period (Yoshinari 2018, Chapter 8).

Moreover, I could not discuss the importance of the moon sufficiently in this work, although the Japanese and Ainu have often worshiped the moon more frequently than the sun (Chapters 2 and 3). At the Sannai Maruyama Site 山内丸山 in Aomori Prefecture, one of the most famous settlement sites of the Jomon Period, a large wooden structure has been reconstructed. Some archaeologists believed that the structure was aligned toward the sunrise. Recently, however, another possibility has been proposed that the structure was aligned to the major standstill of the moon near winter solstice (Hojo Yoshitaka, personal communication).

In addition, *teda* has been commonly considered to refer to the sun in Ryukyu Island archaeology and this term is a symbolic expression of political authority (Chapter 8). There is an opinion, however, that the concept of *teda* actually referred to the moon and that the moon was the most important constellation in ancient Japan (Miura 2008).

Since the moon is the issue that has been least explored in the cultural astronomy of the Japanese Archipelago, I intend to address this issue further in another book at a later time.

References

Miura, Shigehisa 三浦茂久
    2008   *The Worship of the Moon and Regeneration Thought in Ancient Japan.* 『古代 日本の月信仰と再生思想』. Tokyo: Sakuhin-sha.

Oka, Masao 岡正雄
    1979   *Strangers and Others: The Origins of the Japanese People and Culture, and the Formation of Japanese State.* 『異人その他： 日本民族＝文化の源流と日本 国家の形成』. Tokyo: Gensosha.

Yoshinari, Naoki 吉成直樹
    2018   *Kingship and King of the Sun in Ryukyu.* 『琉球王権と太陽の王』 Tokyo: Shichigatsusha.

Index

Page numbers in **bold** denote tables, those in *italics* denote figures.

abnormal burials 69, 116
agricultural: activities, appropriate seasons for 9; calendar, movements of sunrise during 74; economy in Ryukyu Islands 121
agriculture: *Gusuku* Period 121; predicting changes in 51; star for (the Pleiades) 14, 45
Ainu 39; afterworld and funeral customs 112; alignments with Venus, Polaris, Ursa Major 39; bear ceremony (*iomante*) 106, 116; bear hunting 106; beliefs and myths 3; cosmology 117; dialect and material culture 117; grave poles 112–13; groups, dialects of 38; groups, regional 113; homeland 66; hunter-gatherer population 2, 9, 38; hunting territory 108; indigenous hunter-gatherers 63; language 106–8; legend concerning Venus and Mercury 40; local groups 112; name for Big Dipper 41; name for Polar Star 107; observed seasonal movement of sun 107; orientation system 106–7; society 105; star lore 39; traditions 139; view of Gemini 46; villages 4, 103, 107; worshiped the moon 139
Ainu burial orientations: modern **114, 115**; Pre-Modern 4, 113, *115*, 116, 139
Ainu culture 66, 105; ancestor of 104; Center 38; Museum *43*; Preservation Council 105–6; regional variation 117
Ainue houses (*chise*) *105*, 108, *111*; sacred window in 111–12; structure, Pre-Modern 139; Pre-Modern orientation 4
Ainu legend 42, 44; name for Altair 44; name for Arcturus 43; name for constellation Leo 42; name for Orion 45; name for Scorpio 44; star index for seasonal activities 41; star legends depicting bears 42; subsistence 45; view of Cassiopeia 44; view of Sirius 45–6
Ainu people 2–3; homelands 38; house orientation 108; lifestyles, traditional and modern 39; name for spring constellation Leo 42
Ainu, Pre-Modern 108; burial orientation 4, 113, 139; customs 66, 69; dwelling orientation 4; house structure 139
Aldebaran 21, 29, **58–9**, 89
align/alignment: with celestial north of *Soshuku Kofun* 80; of *gusuku* 139; of *Hirabaru* Site 74; of *Jomon* settlements 74; major stars 19; of palaces of local chiefs 126; shrines 28; of stone circles 4, 74, 139; temple 84; of temples at *Yoshinogari* Site settlement 76; of wooden structure at *Sannai Maruyama* Site 139–40

Amano Yasukawara 100
Amaterasu Ohmikami 3, 28; hiding in a rock-dwelling 24; lured from cave 25, 29
animism 9, 139
archaeoastronomical: issues in Japan 84; research/studies 4
archaeoastronomy: in Japan 4, 66; leading figure 67; modern 64; pioneer in Japan 66; in terms of solar phenomena 139
archaeological sites 63, *109*, *122*
archaeologists 126, 140; analysis of burial pole types 112; excavation of *Yoshinogari* Site 76; Japanese 4, 66, 76–7; research grants offered to interdisciplinary projects 5; southern aspect of *kofun* well-known to 64; study of stone circles 71
Arcturus 13, 43–4
Aries 80
astrology 11; astrologer 96; astrological rituals 1; founder of 93
astronomy: paleo-astronomy 1
August Descent from Heaven 28, *30*

beliefs: among the Ainu 3; avoid direction of sacred mountain 111; Big Dipper 41; in Bodhisattva Myoken 10; forgers descended from heaven 100; human life span determined by Polaris and Southern Pole Star 52; indigenous 136; about Mercury 40; in Myoken and in Hokuto, merged 11; Myoken, relevance to ironwork 100; *ona-rigami* (women more sacred than men) 134; in personal guardian star 11; about the Pleiades 45; related to Esoteric Buddhism 4; related to stars 10; religious 1; Shinto 2; that sunlight causes dead to resurrect 66; about the sun, local 137; *teda-ga-ana* (hole of the sun) 126; about tomb in *Urasoe* Castle 128; traditional 3; traditional in Ryukyu Islands 49; turning of heaven and earth 26; *see also* folklore/folktales, myths, oral history
Big Dipper 10, 41–2, 53, **59**; image of 78, *79*; important for gamblers 11; movement of 113; position important for fishermen 21; seven stars/seven-days-star 11, 17, 41, 50–1
Boötes 13, 42–3
Buddhism, Esoteric 1–2, 4, 11, 17, 27, 99; founder of 93; influence of 3, 9, 49; mixed with Shintoism, Confucianism, and indigenous animistic folk beliefs 9, 139
burial mounds: ancient 63; image of Big Dipper 78, *79*; main axis 74, 76; Main, *Hirabaru* site *75*; Main, *Yoshinogari* site *77*; orientation, regularity of 78; temporal shift of orientation 77
burial orientations 4, 113, *115*; clusters corresponding to social units 70; differences by clan 67; at *Genjodaira* Site *71*; in Hokkaido Sites *68*; interpretations of 70; at Jomon sites and shell mounds 66, 69–70; *kofun*, interpretations of 78; northwestern and southeastern in Hokkaido 67; of Pre-Modern Ainu 113, **114**, *115*, 139; regional variation in 116–17; related to direction of sacred *Karosan* Mountain 69; relationship with topography 67, 78; from *Sanganji* Shellmond 69, *70*; sunset points between summer and winter solstices 69; temporal shift related to astronomical ideology 67

Canopus 19, 30, 52
Cassiopeia 9, 17, 20, 44
Centaurus 49–52, 74
child of the sun 4, 126, 128, 132, 136
circumpolar: Big Dipper becomes 41; movement of Big Dipper 113; stars painted in *Soshoku Kofun* 80
cosmology 3, 9; Ainu 117; royal, of Ryukyu Kingdom 137
Crux 49–50, 52
cultural activities 22; astronomical activity 2, 5; diversity 2, 139; Museum, *Ainu 43*; Property Preservation Office, *Hokkaido* 111; and religious factors incorporated into star lore 2; revival movement 39; traditions 9, 139

cultural astronomy in Japan 1, 22; of Hokkaido 2; the moon 140; rich tradition of 5, 139; of Ryukyu Islands 3; studies related to Esoteric Buddhism 2

eclipse 89; solar 25
equinox 106; autumn 84, 107; sunrise point (*cupkarantom*) 46, 76, 107; sunrise and sunset 74; sunset point (*cuppokramtom*) 107; vernal 80, 84, 107
ethnic/minority groups 3, 9, 26

fallen star legends 4, 99, 101; closely related to introduction of advanced forging technology 93; in old literature 89; shrines and temples 90, 92, *94–5*, 96, *98*
fallen stars 93; remnants worshiped 4, 90
farmers 3, 32; importance of Orion to 16–17; importance of Pleiades to 14, 17, 53–4; Japanese 9–10, 13; of *Yaeyama* Archipelago 53–4; *see also* agriculture
festival: annual, *Heian* Era 99; Bon (funeral) 16; Omon 2; star 1; *utagaki* 26
fishermen 3, 10–11; important stars for 17; Japanese 13, 19, 41; see Scorpio as fishhook 50; seasonal and navigation stars for 20–1; shrine 94, 96; in western Japan 17
five-days-star (Cassiopeia) 17–18
folk beliefs 4–5; animistic 9
folklore/folktales: about burial with heads to the east 117; concerning the Pleiades 53; concerning Polaris 19; about a fallen star 99; of the *Setouchi* Inland Sea 17; swan maiden 50; about *Urashima Taro* 31
Forge and the Crucible, The: The Origins and Structure of Alchemy 4
forging 100; advanced 93, 96; iron specialists of 91; mercury 99

Gemini 18–21, 46, **58–9**
goddess 26, 50; *Amamiku* or *Amamikyo* created Ryukyu Islands 136;

Amenouzume lured *Amaterasu* from her hiding place 29; gave birth on Taketomi Island 52; highest, *Amaterasu Ohmikami* 3; Izanami 27, 100; Sun-Goddess as chief deity 65
Goto Akira 5, 9, 20, 39, 49, 54, 60, 63, 114–15, 136
Goto Shuichi 76–7
Gowland, William 4, 63–4, 66, 76, 78

Hata Clan 93, 96, 99
Hokkaido Ainu: culture, ancestor of 104; Culture Center 38; culture, regional variation within 105; dialects 38; economy 39; house and burial orientations 117; traditions 139
Hokuto 11
hokuto-shichisei (seven stars in the north) 11, 51
Hoshi Ura (star inlet) 96, 99
house structure orientation: among Hokkaido Ainu 117; of Pre-Modern Ainu 139
Hyades 14–15, 29, 31, 51

inaw 39, 44, 117; crowns 42, *43*; Sacred Altar dedicated by *40*
iron 96; making 91, 100; sand 91; tools 121; work, relevance of Myoken belief to 100
iron forgers (*tatara*)/ironsmiths 4, 99; believed to descend from heaven 100

Japanese 31; ancient 101; archaeoastronomy 4, 66; archaeologists 4, 66, 76–7; archaeology 63, 70; badminton 14, *15*; belief 32; children 1; Chronicles 24; classical scholar 27; contact with 117; customs 78; culture 3, 49, 139; customs 64; dynasty, first 78; Dynasty, foundation of 33; farmers 9–10; fishermen 13; folklore 99; islands 2, 27, 63; *Kofun* studies 76–7; literature 2, 31, 89; modern 100; navigation 10; poems 32; people 3, 10; researchers 5, 70, 78; sailors and fishermen 19; scholars 24, 26; severe employment imposed

Japanese *continued*
by 42; star lore 10, 21; star worship 99; syllable pattern 32; techniques for transporting rocks 64; term for demon 114; *Tokugawa* government 49; trading with 39; traditional hand drum 16; traditional lunar calendar 18; traditions 9; use of true north and magnetic north 85; war/battle against 39, 44; woman, marriage to 66; wine 84; worship of the moon 139
Japanese, naturalized 100–1; citizen 66; Hata Clan 99
Japanese Archipelago 2, 8; cultural astronomy 3, 5, 139–40; diverse cultural traditions 9; diversity of conception of sky and universe 3; names of Pleiades 51; seasonality of subsistence activities 8; stone circles and monuments 74
Jomon burial orientation and shell mounds 66, 69–70; culture 63; Landscape Studies 74; people 66–7, 74; settlements, alignment of 74; stone circles 70
Jomon Period 63; Late/Final 67, 71; settlement sites 139; stone circles, alignment of 4; stone circles and burials, alignment of 139; *see also* Post-Jomon

Kingdoms of Japan, early fourteenth century 121–2; Central Kingdom 122, 137; Northern Kingdom 122, 130; Southern Kingdom 122, 130
Kitora Kofun 80, *81*; star chart 82
Kofun (tumuli) 63; burial orientations, interpretations of 78, *79*; *Ishizuyama* 78, *79*; orientations 4; Period 63, 76, *79*, 80; *Soshoku* (decorated) 80, *81*, 82; structure and orientation 76; studies 66–7; *Takamatsu Zuka* 80, 82; *see also* burial mounds, *Kitora Kofun*
Kudaka Island *127*, 128, 130, *131*, 132, 134, *135*, 136–7
Kyushu Islands 9, 14, 19, 27, 30, 36, 74, 76, 80, 122

Leo 42–3
Lockyer, N. 64–5

magnetic north 67, 84–5, 114
Meoto Iwa 64
mercury (element of) 99; used in decorating Buddha statues 96
Mercury (planet): daughter of Venus and portent for fishing 40
meteorites 4, 36, 99–100; relationship to forging 100
Milky Way (*Amanogawa*) 1, 44–5, 51–2, 100
mineral resources 96; influenced by astronomical phenomena 4; originated from heaven 99
mines 100; *Benga* 134–5; copper 96; developers 99; developing 93; Silver 93; temples built near 99
mining 99; industry 99–100; technology, teaching 63
Munro, Neil 4, 66, 71
Myoken belief 11; relevance to ironwork 100
Myoken: *Bodhisattva* 10, 90–1, 99; *Hoshida Myoken* Temple *12*; Hoshida Shrine 93, *94*; moved to Buddhist *Juto* Temple 91; Mt. *Hoshida* 93; north, direction of 96; personification of Polar Star 11, 27; star-worship rituals 90; symbolizes Polar Star 93
mythical age of the *Kojiki* and the *Nihonshoki* 33
mythological 24; Age 33; hidden sun motif 25
myths/mythology 49; Ainu people's, of stars 3; ancient 3, 17, 24–5, 100; August Descent from Heaven *30*; creation 131, 134, 136; Japanese 3, 24–5, 49; about the Pleiades 53; result of astronomical phenomena 3; from several clans 24; of stars 2; swan maiden 53

Naka Gusuku Castle 123, *124*
north-south line 108; *Asuka* Period 34; chain of Japanese Archipelago 2; fundamental axis for city planning in China 33–4; seasonality of subsistence activities 8; temples were built along 84
north, true 36, 67, 84–5, 114

observation of stars 1–2, 56–7, 82; astronomical 33; used for everyday life 3
Okinawa 48; beliefs about human life span 52; *Denshowa Shiryo* Center 50, 53, 56; Island 4, 135; Main Island 50, 57, 121, *122*; name for Pleiades 51; name for Scorpio 13; Prefecture 9, 122; turtle shell burials 49
Okinawan people 49, 52; indigenous astronomy of 3; name for Vega 50; solar ideology in folk beliefs among 4; star lore 2
Omoro-soshi chants 52, 122–3, 128, 132, 134, 136
oral history: of Ainu people 108; Research Center, Okinawa 6; Ryukyu Islands 3, 49; *Tokachi* Region 117
Orion 3, 9–10, 45; acronical rise 17; *Amenouzume who is dancing* 29; direction-telling star 17; heliacal rise 16; navigational constellation in ancient Japan 27; Orion's Belt 14, 17, 21, 27–9, 45, 51, **58–9**; Orion's Blade 29

Palaeolithic Period 63
Pegasus 44–5, **58–9**
Pisces, vernal equinox close to 80
pit: burials 76; dwelling site *116*
Pleiades 31, 45, 51–2, **58–9**; guide for agriculture 14–17, 54; eight crossroads of heaven 29; folktale concerning 53; guide for fishing seasons 20–1; observation of 53, 60, 136; shrine 3, 56; *subaru-boshi* 9; used for knowing direction and weather 10
Polaris/Northern Polar Star (*nenufa-bushi*) 10–11, 26, 41, 78, 84; folktale concerning 19–20; importance in Chinese city planning 33; influence on human life span 52; less important to Ainu 107; shines behind main architectural axis of *Kitano Tenmangu* 36; symbolized by *Myoken* 27, 93, 99; symbol lacking from *SankouMon* Gate 36; used for navigation 19, 39, 51–2, 93; worship of 36, 133
poles: boys and girls circle around 26; burial/grave 112–13, 117; burial, female/women's 112–13; burial, male 112; *kadomatsu/matsugui* (pine) 18–20
Polynesians 13, 107; sacred power (*mana*) 126; saw Scorpio as a fishhook 50
Post-Jomon: culture 103–4; Period 67, 69
Prehistoric Japan 66
priest Bin (Buddhist) 89
priestess 134; access to shrine 135; introduced sunlight/*sezi* to sacred place 126, 134; rituals held before December solstice to initiate 130; of royal palace, daughter of founder of *Kudaka* Island 131; stars seen as 44; sun 74; supplying sacred power to the king 136

religious beliefs 1; context of Cassiopeia 17; factors in star lore 2; five-days-star/seven-days-star 17–18; life 49; object shaved from a willow branch (*inaw*) 42; practices 1; role taken by women 134; shrines 56; specialists, men and women 49; structures 76; thought 137; traditions 9
rituals: annual 53; astrological 1; from China, December solstice 133; grounds 76; places or burials 71; star-worship 90
rituals of the Ainu 44; *inaw* used in 39, 42; iomante 106; killing 106; seasonal, performed during vernal and autumnal equinoxes 107; *sinnorappa* and *iacrapa* 107; worship of Venus 39
rituals of the Ryukyu Islands: in February and June of lunar calendar 131; new year 133; to remove harmful insects 130; *Izaiho* 130; of receiving sunlight 134; remnant 136; royal 136–7; succession 135; sun 4, 135; worship of the sun 132

Index

rock(s): coral 128; divided, sacred space behind 135; fragments of fallen stars 93, *94*, 96, *97*; give orientation for shrine of adoration 65; *gusuku* gate constructed with 123; *Hanareji 127*; heavy, Japanese techniques to transport 64; Husband-Wife (*Meoto Iwa*) 64; *Masuda Iwafune* 82; sacred 49, 74, *97*, *135*; *Sakafune Ishi* 84; splitting god 100; symbolic meaning of 65; Tametomo (separated) 128; transformation of a star 90; *Ugan-jima* 131

rock-dwelling 24–5; Cave of Heaven 29

Ryukyu Islanders 9; beliefs of 130; rich star lore 136; traditions of cultural astronomy 139; used celestial and natural phenomena to predict seasonal/weather changes 51; used rising/setting points of stars for compass points 57; view of stars as sacred objects 52

Ryukyu Islands 14, *48*; called Okinawa Prefecture now 122; creation myth 134, 136; cultural astronomy 2–3; earliest human occupation of 121; importance of the Pleiades 53; indigenous orientation system 123; Kudaka Island 130; legend 126; lie in northern hemisphere 51; observation of rise and fall of stars 60; religion 49; religious shrines (*utaki*) 56; sub-tropical zone 9; traditional belief and oral history in 3, 49; turtle shell burial type 49; unpublished folk tales 6; women held to be more sacred than men 134

Ryukyu Kingdom 122; founded by chiefly clans of *Urasoe* Castle 126; *Gusuku* Period 121; independent 9, 48; Origin of 135; prospered through trade 49; royal cosmology in 137; royal ritual of 136; solar ideology in 4, 139; united local powers 121

sacred window 106; orientation of 108–9, *110*, 111–12, 117; use in bear ceremony (*iomante*) 106

Sagittarius 51

sailors 3; custom of observing stars 10; importance of Big Dipper for 10–11; importance of Cassiopeia 17; importance of Orion's Belt 17; Japanese 19; name for Corvus 13

Satsumon culture 69, 104–5, 116–17

Scorpio 13–14, 44, 50

Seven-Days Stars 17–18; seven small stars 41; worshiped *11*

seven stars 50; design *11*; in the north (Big Dipper) perceived as seven deities 11, 51, 54; position/angle indicate time for catching tuna 21; in the south (Sagittarius) 51, 54; swan maiden folktale 50; of Urso Minor 41

shaman 44; sacred zone for 49; shamanism 9, 49

Shell Mound Period 121

shell mounds: Esan 69; *Jomon* 66; *Moyoro 109*, *116*; *Sanganji* 69; *Takasago* 69; *Tzugumo* 66

shells: Foraminifera star sand 52; turtle shell burials 49

Shikoku Island 9, 17, 20, 96

Shinto beliefs 2, 139; cult, ancient 65; entrances 49; shrines 4, 64, 74, 90

Shintoism 3, 9, 49

shrine(s) 36; *Amatsumikahoshi* 30; *Daishogun 11*; established by Hata Clan from China 93; of fallen star legend 90, 94, 96; fishermen visit to ensure good catch 96; gods of *Iwasaku* 100; *Hoshida Myoken* 93, *94*; *Hosoya* and *Hoshiya* 93; *Ise* 3, 64, 74; Kanawa 91, *92*; *Kitano Tenmangu 36*; Kudamatsu 91, *92*; Land God 34; meteorite 99; *Misaki Utaki* 53; Pleiades 3, 56; related to fallen star legend, Hoshio and Takaboshi 95; rocks that fell from heaven 96; sacred 121; Shinto 4, 64, 74, 90; star tail 94; *Sumiyoshi 28*; traditional (utaki) 49; true star 96; to worship *Bodhisattva Myoken* 91; *see also utaki*

shrine(s) alignment/orientation 28, 65; originally facing south, changed to face north 94, 96

Index 147

Shuri 126; district 132; Dynasty 132, 134–6; Kingdom of 4; Royal Palace 50, 126; solar kingdom in 132, 134, 136; trading route with China 57
Shuri Castle *122*, 126, 130, 132, *133*, 134, 136; Royal 133
six stars 41, 45
solar 139; disc, first appearance of 76; dynasty 128; eclipse 25; ecliptic 84; ideology, development in Ryukyu Kingdom 4, 128, 139; king 132; kingdom in Shuri 132; kingship 136
solstice, summer: *icharupa* ceremony held 39; rising point, Gemini north of 46; market 99; rising point of sun 106; rituals 107; sunrise 9; sunrise behind *Aguni* Island *61*; sunrise, enclosed settlement axis alignment 76; sunrise at *Meoto Iwa*, worship of 64; sunrise and sunset directions *68*, 107
solstice, winter: burial orientation in Hokkaido Sites *68*, 69; market 99; return of sun from 46; rise of Orion 17, 46; rising point of the sun 106; standstill of the moon 140; sunrise behind *Kudaka-jima* Island *127*; sunrise and sunset points 46, 107; sunset, enclosed settlement axis 76
southeast: coast of Okinawa Island, *Seifa-Utaki* 135; from Shuri Royal Castle, gates located 133; from Tametomo Rock, winter solstice seen 128
southeast Asia: cultures from 48, 139; trade with 49, 121–2
southeast burial orientations: in Hokkaido 67; of the Pre-Modern Ainu 113–14
southern: China 49; Cross 74; Hokkaido 41; orientation of burial chambers 64, 78; Osaka 28; Polar Star 52; region 41; Ryukyu Islands of Japan 2, 9; Seven Stars 54; side of the house, sacred window located in 111; star, Centaurus 51; Yaeyama Archipelago 57
southern Kingdom of Japan 122, 130; Satsuma clan of Kyushu Island 122
Southern Polar Star 52
southern Sakhalin 112; Ainu 38, 114; Ainu, burials of 116; Okhotsk culture originated in 104
southern sky: banishment to 54; bright stars seen in 50; Corvus seen in 21; *Kitora Kofun* star chart 82; position of Scorpio in 13
south, true *36*
star books 9; Tarama Island 56–7
star charts/maps 3, 49; from *Hateruma* Island 57, *60*; indigenous 56; *kofun* painted with 80, *81*, 82; Micronesian 57; of Ryukyu Islanders 9; Chinese, *Soshoku Kofun* painted with 82
star clusters 14, 51–3
star lore 2–3; Ainu tradition 9, 39; indigenous star book of Tarama Island 56; Japanese 9–10, 21–2; Ryukyu Island 136
star shrine(s) 91, 93–4, 99–100; constructed near mines 99; *Hoshi Jinja* 96, *97–8*, 99–100; *Manaboshi* 96, *98*, 99; of northern Kanto 100; *Takaboshi Jinja*, *Myojinsha* and *Manaboshi Jinja* 96, *97–8*
star worship 93, 99, 99, 101; on basis of Chinese star customs 93; rituals 90
stone circles 67, 74; geometrical analysis of 71; Jomon 70; of Jomon Period, alignment of 4, 139; Ohyu, in Akita 70, *72*; Oshoro 66, 71, *73*; specialized burial 66; sundials of Jomon Era 70
sunrise: direction 106, 108, 111, 117–18; gusuku gate 123, 125; behind Hinata Pass *75*; influence on house and burial orientation 4; light through sacred window 108; movement during agricultural calendar 74; observation of stars 57; orientation for 66; points at solstices *110*; sacred direction 130; Sannai Maruyama Site wooden structure aligned 139–40; at solstices and equinoxes 74, 76, 107; at *teda-ga-ana* 130; winter solstice 46, 60
sunrise, summer solstice 9, 60, *61*, *65*, 107; behind Aguni Island *61*; burial orientation in Hokkaido Sites *68*;

sunrise, summer solstice *continued*
  castle gates reconstructed to face 136; enclosed settlement axis 76; from *Futamiga-ura*, Ise 64, *65*; ritual, *miruku-gwati* 131; worship of 64
sunrise, winter solstice: direction *68*; enclosed settlement axis 76; behind *Kudaka-jima* Island *127*; observation of 60; rising point of the sun 106–7; Sirius rises at 46
sunset: burial orientation ranges 69; point 5000 years ago, orientation of 71; at solstices *110*; at solstices and equinoxes 74, 107; stars observed at 57; *suji-kai* stars in western sky after 17
sunset direction 4, 106, 117; Ainu believe afterworld lies in 112; considered impure by Ryukyu Islanders 130
sunset, summer solstice: direction *68*; mention rare in Shuri Dynasty Period 136; point 71
sunset, winter solstice: direction *68*; enclosed settlement axis 76; point 46, 107
sun worship 63–4, 67, 70, 78, 132
surveying technology/techniques 63

Tamagusuku Castle *125*
Taurus 3, 31, **58–9**, 80
teda-ga-ana (hole of the sun) 126, 128; sun rises at 130

Urasoe Castle 126, *127*, 128; chiefly lineage 126, 132; Dynasty 128, 130, 135–7; Gusuku *122*; Yodore 128, *129*
Ursa Major 41–2
utaki (traditional shrines) 49; Benga Mine 134–5; *Muribushi* (the Pleiades) *56*; *Misaki 53*; *Seifa* 122, *135*

Vega (*chura aguâ bushi*) 1, 50
Venus 1, 30, 41, 52; and Mercury, legend concerning 40; as morning star 31, 39; use in navigation 20–1, 39; visible during daytime 89; worshiped for ritual reasons 39

women 131, 137; accessories buried with 113; Ainu 45; dancing (Big Dipper) 41; direction of turning 26; officials, using gates southeast of palace 133; shape of burial poles for 112–13; taboo of touching 100; viewed as religious specialists/more sacred than men 49, 134
worshippers 65
worship/worshiped: *Amaterasu* 3; *Amatsumikahoshi*, as principle god 30; ancestral spirits 107; Bodhisattva *Myoken* 91, 99; December solstice and *Kudaka* Island 137; gods, three brothers 27–8; *Iwa-saku* and *Nesaku* 100; king, as child of the sun 4; *Kokuzo-Bosatsu* 99; *Kudaka* Island 134–5; the moon 139; north direction 133; phallic 64; the Pleiades 56; Polaris/Polar Star 36, 93; Polaris and Forbidden City of Beijing 133; remnants of fallen stars 4, 90; sacred place 121; Seven-Days Stars *11*; stars 93–4, 101; stone/meteorite (fallen star) 99–100; of summer solstice sunrise 64; sun 60, 63–4, 67, 70, 78, 132, 134; Venus 39

Yayoi Period 63; settlement studies 74, 76
Yoshinogari Site 76, *77*

zodiac: animals 57; Chinese traditions/system 11, 31, 57; signs 11